People
AND THE
Natural
Environment

SERIES EDITOR: BOB WALTON

Chris Martin

HODDER AND STOUGHTON

LONDON SYDNEY AUCKLAND TORONTO

CONTENTS

Plate margins

As the plates drift about they form various features at their edges or margins. The type of features formed depends upon
– the thickness of the plates (at between 15–30 km, continental plates are much thicker than oceanic plates which may be only 5–6 km thick);
– the speed of the movement.

Creating new crust

Figure 1.3 shows that as the plates pull apart molten rock from inside the Earth can seep up and reach the surface. This is known as a constructive margin. This cools and forms new crust.

Fig. 1.4 *Volcanoes in Lanzarote*

Fig. 1.3 *A constructive margin*

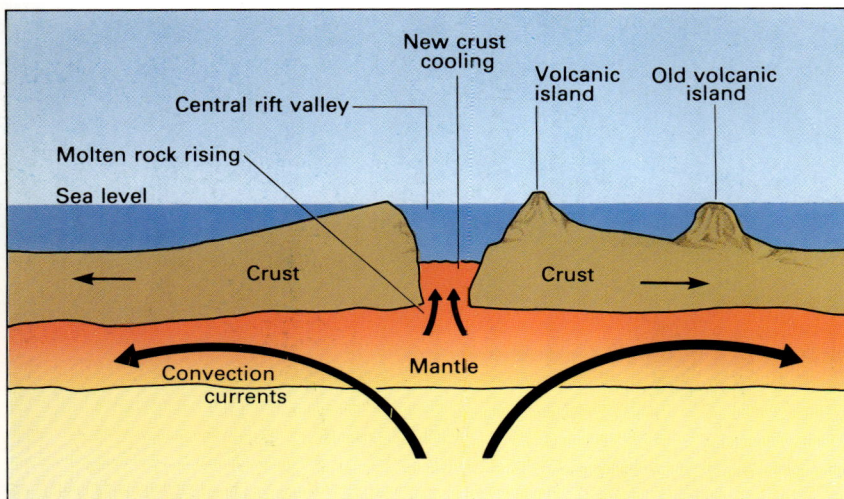

Sometimes this type of margin is still preserved in volcanic islands. The photograph (fig. 1.4) shows a line of volcanoes in Lanzarote which marks the position of a constructive margin.

Fig. 1.5 *The Southern Atlantic*

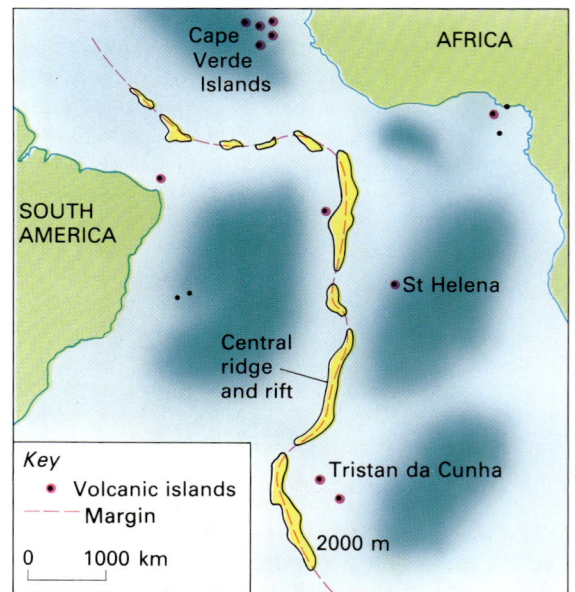

Activities

1 Look at figure 1.3. Why do you think that this margin is called constructive? Why are so many volcanic islands formed at such a margin?
2 There is a central rift valley along the ridge formed as the plates move apart. What is a rift valley and why do you think it forms here?
3 Measure the approximate distance away from the margin of each of the volcanic islands shown in fig. 1.5. Draw a diagram of your findings placing the distances in order. What pattern does this produce?

Destroying crust

Look at fig. 1.6 which shows two types of colliding 'destructive' margins. The type and amount of destruction depends on the thickness of each of the colliding plates. If two thick and strong continental plates collide then mountains are buckled up (fig. 1.6A). If one of the plates is a thin denser oceanic plate then it is pushed under and down by the thicker but lighter continental plate (fig. 1.6B) and so it forms an oceanic trench, as shown in fig. 1.7. The bending of this plate may lead to the formation of a line of offshore volcanic islands as weaknesses allow molten rock to reach the surface. Examples of both types of collisions include the Himalayas (where two thick plates collide) and off the west coast of South America (where two weak plates collide).

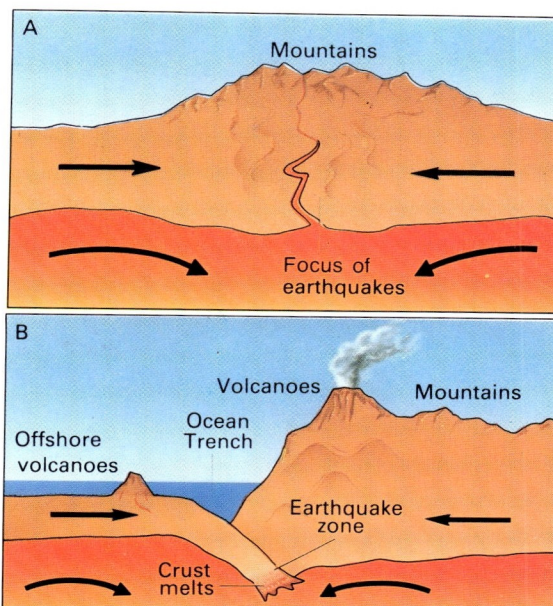

Fig. 1.6 *Destructive margins*

Fig. 1.7 *Part of the west coast of South America*

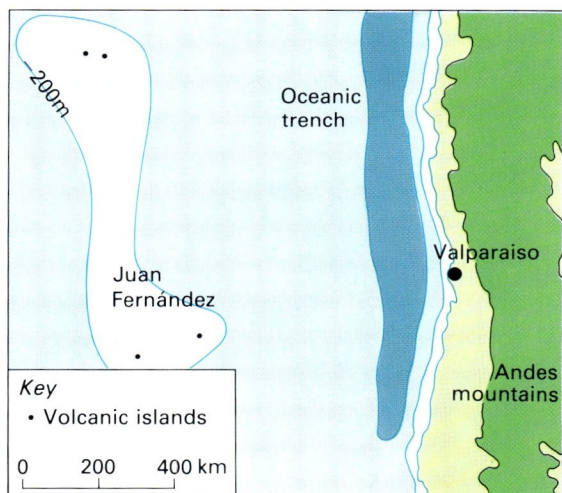

Causing earthquakes

The type of margin where plates slide past each other is called a conservative margin. The map (fig. 1.8) shows the San Andreas margin in California which is one of the most rapidly sliding margins. Currently the western side is moving northwards at about 7 cm a year. This is not a smooth movement but happens in a series of jerks, which to us are earthquakes. The map of the San Francisco area suggests why such an earthquake would be so disastrous. All the plates are linked so one type of movement triggers off others. On 19 September 1985 an earthquake hit Mexico City and two months later a volcano erupted 3200 km further south. Both were disasters!

Fig. 1.8 *Major Californian fault lines*

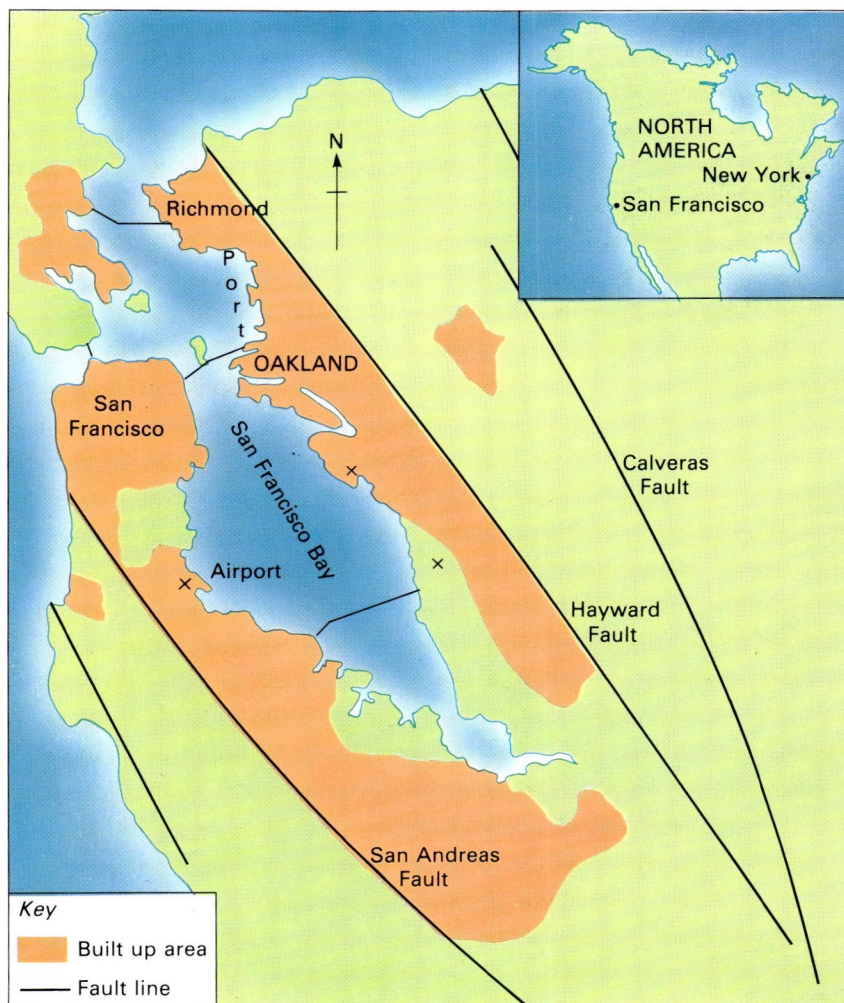

The hazards of earthquakes

As plates slide past or into each other they do so in sudden jerks or shocks. These are called earthquakes and most originate deep in the crust. The point on the Earth's surface above the actual earthquake centre is called the epicentre. The shock waves may travel at 25 000 km/hour, as in the case of the 19 September 1985 Mexican earthquake.

The exact nature of the damage produced by such sudden shocks depends on the size, the depth of the shock, the distance from the shock and the type of surface landscape. Why did the Mexico earthquake of 1985 at a force of 8.2 on the Richter scale cost eighty times more lives than the 1964 Alaskan quake which rated a force of 8.4? Earthquakes produce hazards both directly and indirectly. Figure 1.10 shows a map of the typical hazards, and how some of the damage in zone 2 can slow down the help trying to reach the main area of damage.

Fig. 1.9 *Building design*

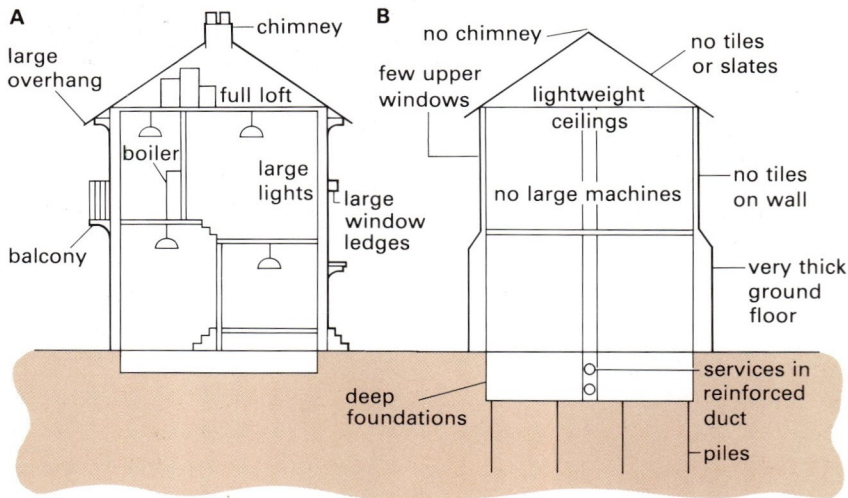

Building damage

The shock waves knock down weak buildings and may make more resistant buildings vibrate, causing windows to shatter and tiles to fall off.

Fig. 1.10 *Earthquake hazards. Draw a cross-section of these hazards, clearly labelling the epicentre and the different levels of damage.*

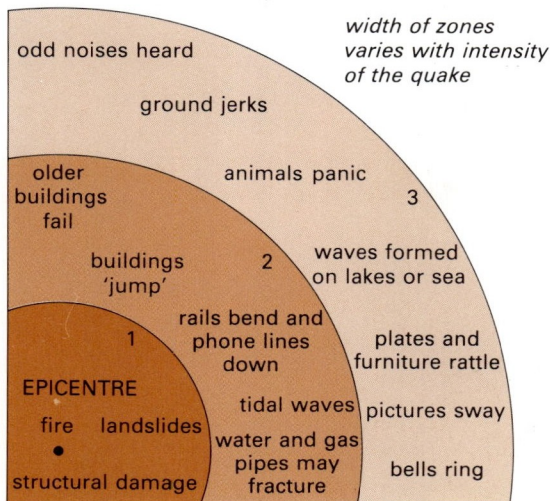

Activities

Compare the two buildings in fig. 1.9.
1 Make a list of the ways building B is safer in the shock of an earthquake than building A.
2 Why are poor or developing countries such as Mexico more at risk to such damage?
3 Second or third shock waves cause more deaths and destruction despite being weaker than the first – can you explain why? In Mexico in 1985 over 9000 died and 95 000 were made homeless.

Disruption of services

Earthquake shocks may burst gas mains and start fires. In the 1923 Tokyo earthquake fire destroyed 300 000 buildings, which made up approximately two-thirds of the city. Other services such as electricity lines might also be damaged and so encourage the spread of fire. Again this danger is more of a problem in the cities of developing countries. Famine and disease can also result as food supplies are lost and drains damaged. In the 1964 Alaskan earthquake, pipelines from the Seward refinery were broken. This created more than one hazard in the area by adding pollution to the hazard of fire.

Tidal waves (tsunamis)

If an earthquake occurs either under the sea or near the coast then the shock waves are turned into large sea waves that devastate the low lying coastal areas. In the Alaskan earthquake the tsunamis were 9 m high and they wrecked the port of Valdez.

Disruption of communications

The Alaskan earthquake damaged 25% of the roads and over 50% of the bridges had to be rebuilt. Runways were cracked and rail tracks buckled or broken, making the initial task of rescue and aid more difficult. It is difficult to say who should pay for this 'Act of God'.

Landslides

Vast cracks may open up and new cliffs may be created by the earth movements. In Alaska a 2 km stretch of cliff slid down 20–30 m taking seventy buildings with it. What other problems do you think landslides could cause?

Fig. 1.11 *Earthquake damage, Alaska*

Human activity

Human activity can create earthquakes, for example, by nuclear testing, mining and the building of reservoirs. A new lake formed may be so heavy that it sets off crustal movements. When Lake Kariba on the Zambesi was filled in 1958, 2000 tremors were set off reaching a force of 5.8.

Fig. 1.12 *Extract from an earthquake preparation leaflet given to people living in part of California*

1. Have flashlights and portable radio with extra batteries.
2. Have first-aid kit and fire extinguisher.
3. Store a few gallons of water per family member.
4. Have one week's food stored outside the house.
5. Strap down boiler.
6. Do not place beds anywhere near windows or mirrors.
7. Have a plan to reunite the family, day or night.

Activities

Look at figs 1.11 and 1.12. Imagine you are living in the area when the earthquake hits.
1 Why might a fire extinguisher be needed?
2 Why does food need to be stored outside the house?
3 Why should beds be placed away from windows?

Earth movements

Mountains are high areas of land usually over 300 m higher than the surrounding land. Plate movements can create mountains in a number of ways, as shown in the map (fig. 1.13) of South America. The Andes is the longest continuous mountain range in the world extending over 7000 km and rising to nearly 7000 metres. The highest peak is Aconcagua in Argentina at 6960 metres.

Folded mountains

The exact height, size and shape of the mountain depends on the degree of pressure exerted by the colliding plates folding the rocks and on the softness of the rock being folded.

Once fold mountains have been formed they immediately begin to be worn down by ice, rain, rivers and wind. The once smoothly folded strata are broken up and form the typical jagged mountain peaks shown in the photograph (fig. 1.16) of the Alps.

Fig. 1.13 *The Andes*

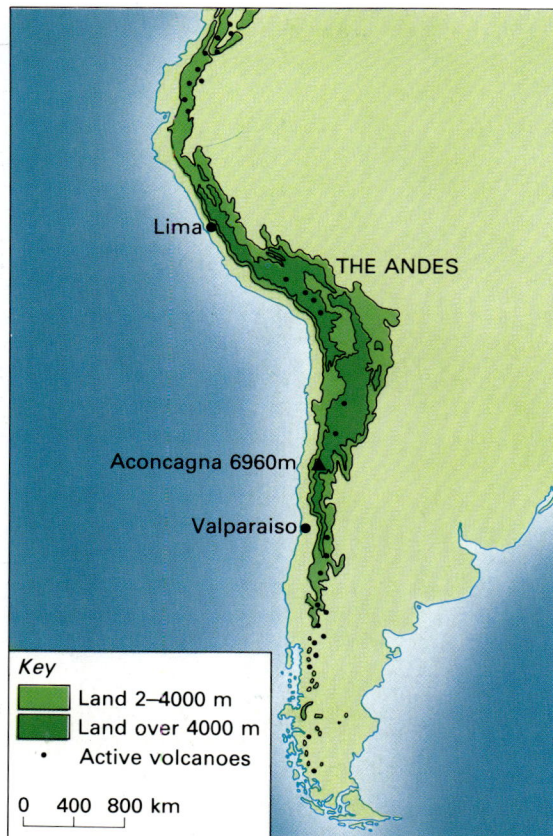

Key

Land 2–4000 m

Land over 4000 m

• Active volcanoes

0   400   800 km

Fig. 1.14 *Types of fold*

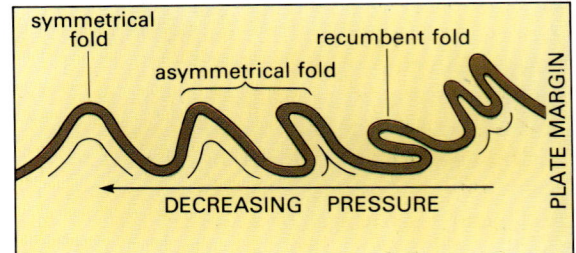

symmetrical fold

asymmetrical fold

recumbent fold

PLATE MARGIN

DECREASING   PRESSURE

Fig. 1.15 *Cliffs at Broad Haven, Pembrokeshire*

Activities

1 Look at fig. 1.14. How does the appearance of the fold vary with distance from the plate margin? Why are the folds formed near to the margins more easily worn away?
2 The photograph (fig. 1.15) shows a cliff section at Broad Haven, Pembrokeshire. How near to the margin do you think this was when it was folded? Draw a fieldsketch of the photograph and add labels for the weaknesses formed by the folding.

Fig. 1.16 *The Alps*

Volcanoes

The exact type of volcanic mountain formed may depend upon several factors.

1 *The type of eruption* The photograph (fig. 1.17) shows a typical volcanic cone in the Andes. These volcanoes sometimes produce high mountains. In the case of a fissure eruption a flat sheet of lava is produced, like the nearly 600 km² sheet from the Laki fissure eruption in Iceland in 1783. These do not form mountains.

2 *The type of material* Some lava is very fluid and flows over a large area forming a flat, shield volcano as shown in fig. 1.18. If eruption follows eruption these can build up to great heights. Mauna Kea in Hawaii is such a volcano and extends over 9000 metres in height from the seabed. Some lava is very sticky and forms smaller dumpy cones that rarely become high mountains. The photograph (fig. 1.19) shows an ash cone in Iceland.

Fig. 1.19 *Ash cone, Iceland. Why do ash cones rarely form tall volcanoes? Suggest why the wind has more influence than water on its shape*

3 *The depth of the volcano* Some lava never reaches the surface but cools deep in the crust. There may be so much lava injected that it pushes up the overlying rocks to form highland as shown in fig. 1.20. In some areas, when the softer surrounding rocks are worn away, the harder injected lava is left as highland.

Fault (or block) mountains

If cracks or faults occur near each other, the ground in between may be forced up to form block mountains. A typical example of this is the Rhine rift valley, where the Vosges block mountains and the Black Forest block mountains rise to over 1400 metres on either side of the rift valley, as shown in fig. 1.21.

Fig. 1.17 *An Andean volcano*

Fig. 1.18 *A shield volcano*

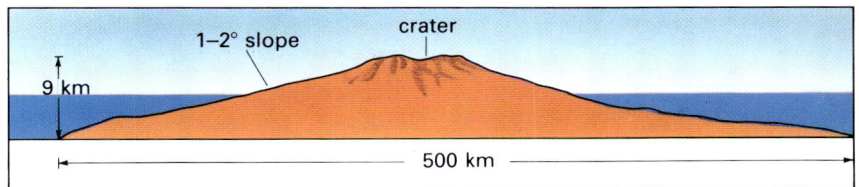

Fig. 1.20 *Intrusive mountain*

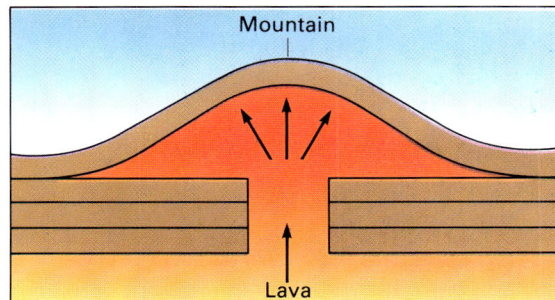

Fig. 1.21 *Fault mountains. How could you tell a block mountain from a fold mountain?*

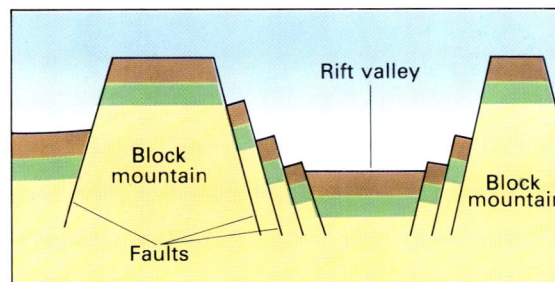

The hazards of volcanic areas

There are over 600 active volcanoes in the world today, over 100 of them in Indonesia. Volcanoes produce various dangers, as shown in fig. 1.22. It can be especially dangerous to live in a valley near a volcano, although the fertility of the soils may make the risk worthwhile. Volcanic hazards may be direct or indirect.

Fig. 1.22 *Volcanic hazards*

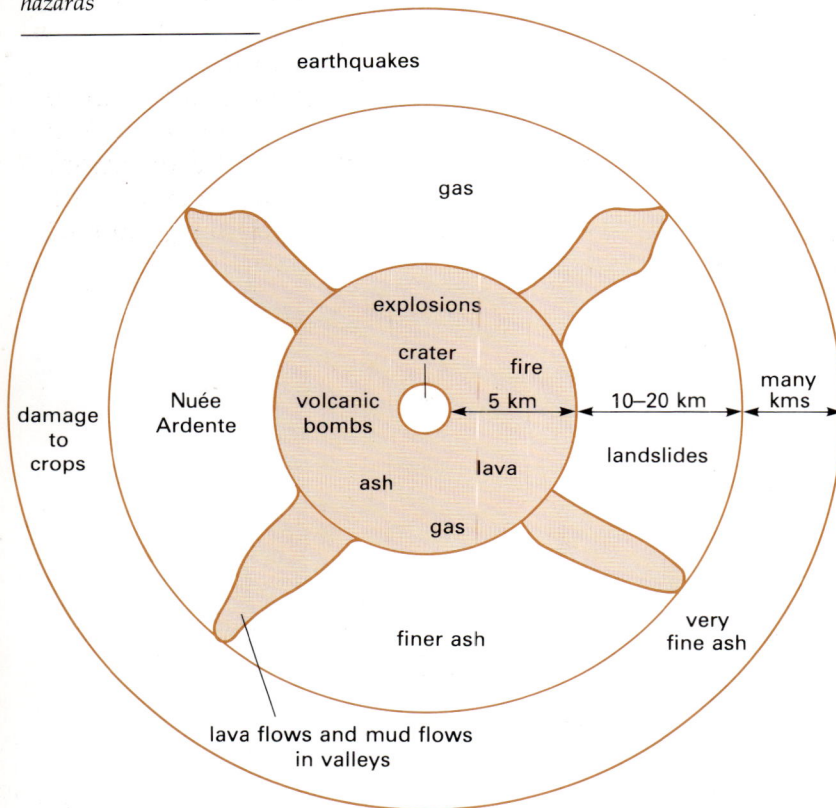

earthquakes

gas

explosions

crater   fire

Nuée   volcanic   5 km   10–20 km   many
Ardente   bombs   kms

damage   landslides
to
crops   ash   lava

gas

finer ash   very
                                   fine ash

lava flows and mud flows
in valleys

The force of the explosion

In 1883 Krakatoa, a volcanic island in Indonesia, exploded producing a cloud 80 km high and destroying the 4000 m high mountain and island. The impact of such a large explosion may generate numerous earthquakes and tsunamis (tidal waves) that swamp coastal areas. The 40 m high tsunamis formed by the Krakatoa eruption drowned the local coastlines and 36 000 people.

The debris

In 1783 Iceland's Laki fissure (a 24 km long crack) erupted spreading lava over 600 km^2 of the best farmland. A lava flow can dam and redirect entire rivers and some lava may flow as fast as 50 km/hour.

Pompeii near Naples in Italy was covered by a thick layer of ash and dust when Mount Vesuvius erupted in 79 AD. Look at fig. 1.23 which shows such an eruption. In the case of Mount St Helens in Washington State, USA that erupted in 1982, the 2 km^3 of ash that fell destroyed over $50 million of crops and $30 million of fruit, especially apples. The ash was so tough that it did great damage to farm machinery as the farmers tried to work the land.

Fig. 1.23 *An ash eruption. Imagine you were a local citizen. Try to describe your feelings as the fine ash starts to fall. Why do you decide to stay rather than leave?*

Gas

Sometimes superheated and poisonous gases are released. These are usually denser than air and roll down the side of the volcano killing all life. In 1902 the city of St Pierre in the West Indies was hit by the eruption of Mount Pelée. A cloud of ash and gas at a temperature over 1000°C rolled down the side of the volcano and killed 30 000 people. Sometimes the gas is poisonous, containing carbon dioxide or sulphur dioxide.

Look at the newspaper article (fig. 1.24).
1 How did the disaster happen?
2 What percentage of the village population died? Why do you think that the death toll was so high?
3 Imagine that you were a rescue worker – what problems would you have faced?

Fire

Volcanic eruptions do not burn things directly but the molten lava is so hot that vegetation, crops and wooden buildings burst into flames. In the 1973 eruption of Heimaey off the southern coast of Iceland, 300 buildings were burnt down and sixty-five buried under ash. Fires caused by volcanoes can spread way beyond the local area.

Storms

The heat and gas released by an eruption sometimes produce vast towering clouds that can lead to thunderstorms. The vast clouds of fine ash may be thrown up so high in the atmosphere that the climate over a large area can be changed. Figure 1.25 shows the area covered by the ash cloud from the Mount St Helens' eruption.

Fig. 1.25 *Ash deposits. Why did the ash go in this direction? What effects might it have had on the climate of the area?*

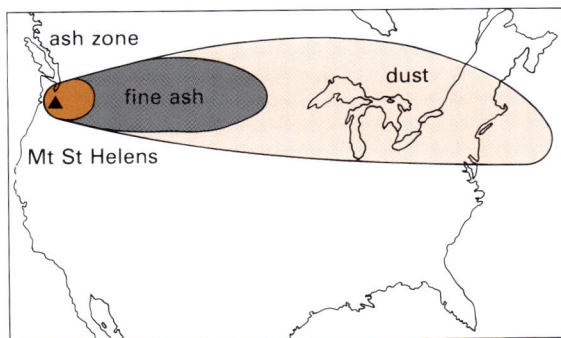

Fig. 1.24 *Disaster at Almeiro*

14 NOVEMBER 1985

DISASTER STRIKES COLOMBIAN TOWN

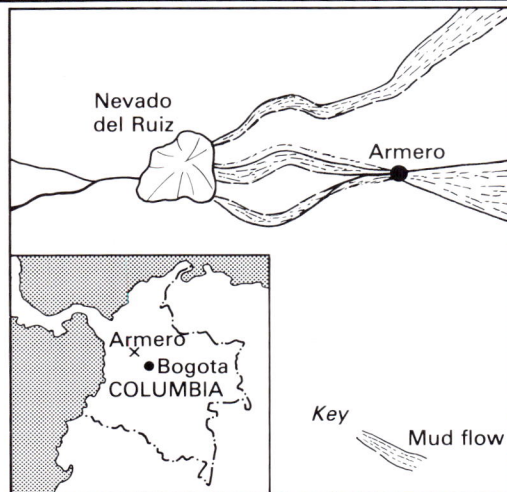

Columbia's volcano Nevado del Ruiz yesterday sent a 140 km/hour, 40 m high, wave of mud and ash through the narrow canyons of the Langunilla River until at 11 pm, without any warning, it swamped the town of Almero 50 km from the eruption. Many were caught in their beds and only 3000 of the town's 23 000 population survived. Most were buried under 3.5 m of warm mud.

Fig. 1.26 *A Volcanic peak*

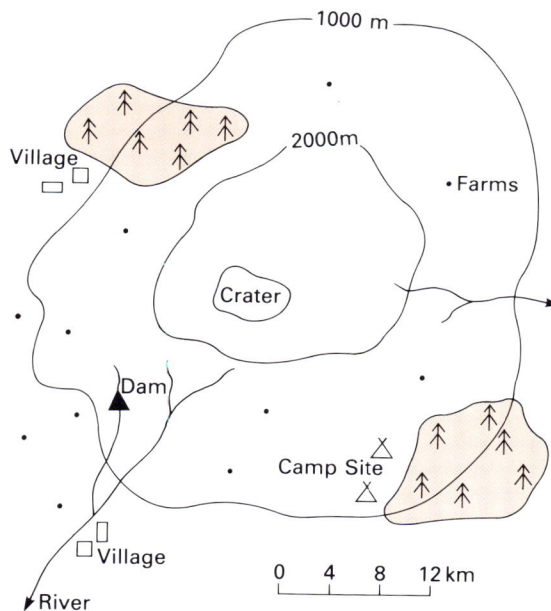

Activities

1 Use the hazards map (fig. 1.22) to predict the hazards for the volcanic peak shown in the map (fig. 1.26). Why might your predictions be wrong?
2 Design a plan to minimise the threat to the village shown in fig 1.26. How might you divert the lava flow? Why might there be opposition to your plan?

The uses of volcanoes

Volcanic 'new land'

Whole islands may be created by eruptions. The eruption of Heimaey in 1973 added 25% extra land to the Icelandic island. Indeed Iceland is itself a creation of volcanoes.

Fertile soils

Volcanic soils are rich in minerals, especially potash and phosphate. This means that areas of old lavas can produce high crop yields and vital foods for densely populated countries like Indonesia.

Minerals

The molten lava often contains gases rich in minerals. These may be injected into cracks to produce mineral veins as the gases cool. Figure 1.27 shows some of the mining areas in the granite rocks of Cornwall and Devon. The chief minerals mined were copper and tin but the veins often contain many other ores such as arsenic, lead sulphide, iron ore and zinc. The photograph (fig. 1.28) shows one of the old engine sheds in Cornwall. These contained the old steam engines that were used to lift the ore and pump out water from the deep mines. Today only two mines are still active as mining is costly and most of the best seams are exhausted.

Fig. 1.27 *Granite areas of Cornwall and part of Devon*

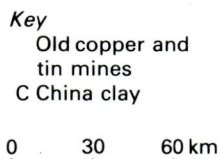

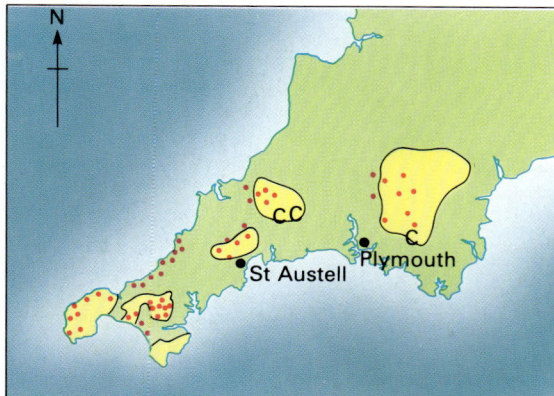

Key
Old copper and tin mines
C China clay

0   30   60 km

Much of the world's copper, gold and silver are found in old volcanic rocks such as the 'Hill of Silver' found at Potosi in Bolivia. Sulphur is one of the major minerals extracted from volcanic areas such as Sicily and Chile. Its chief uses are to make acids, fertilizers, dyes and

Fig. 1.28 *An engine shed near Helston. What effects did this mining have on the landscape?*

synthetic rubber. In tropical areas heavy rainfall may wash the minerals down into the soil and form bauxite. This can be extracted and used to make aluminium. Sometimes rising gases react with granite to form gemstones such as topaz and tourmaline and in South Africa diamonds are found in old volcanic 'pipes'.

Stone

Granite is widely used as a building stone for houses, as road chippings and in a polished form as shop fronts. Look at the table (fig. 1.29) which shows a survey of the building stone used in a typical high street. Another volcanic rock, obsidian, was used to make axes and tools in pre-metal cultures. Volcanic ash is frequently crushed and mixed with cement to produce building blocks.

Fig. 1.29 *High street survey of shop-fronts. Why do banks use volcanic rocks?*

	volcanic	non-volcanic
Banks	6	5
Building societies	4	7
Jewellers	8	4
Chemists	1	5
Total	19	21

Hot water

Fifty-five bore holes in the Reykjavik area of Iceland, shown in fig. 1.31, supply water at 87°C to heat all the houses of a population of over 120 000. There are over fourteen high-temperature fields used and nearly 700 km of pipe, as shown in the photograph (fig. 1.30). This form of heating has little impact on the environment as it involves no burning and the waste product is water.

Fig. 1.30 *Piped steam in Iceland*

Power

Iceland has three electricity-generating plants driven by steam from geysers. The largest is at Krafla (shown in fig. 1.31) which was built in 1979 and now produces 60 MW. The largest geothermal power station is The Geysers in California where 200 wells and fifteen power plants produce 1000 MW. Many other countries are searching for 'hot rocks' to use as a source of clean cheap power. Such schemes usually involve pumping cold water down bore holes which are deep enough to reach the hot areas.

Activities

Study the photograph (fig. 1.32) and the section of a tourist brochure from the Iceland Tourist Board (fig. 1.33).
1 What type of tourist do you think this kind of volcanic area attracts? Make a list of any problems tourists might encounter in visiting such areas.
2 Why is tourism so vital to the Icelandic economy? Draw a suitable poster to attract visitors from wealthy countries.
3 What additional facilities would you have to build for the tourists?

Fig. 1.31 *Iceland.*

Key
- Hotels
- Power station
- Areas of hot springs
- Area of most recent volcanic activity

0 50 100 km

Health spas

Minerals dissolve in the hot water and these can be used to help cure various ailments, especially rheumatism and arthritis. In Britain, Bath is the only thermal spa with water naturally reaching 49°C. Some of these thermal springs have high levels of sulphur, such as Eaux-Bannes in the Pyrenees, while Bath's springs are high in iron.

Fig. 1.32 *One of the many volcanic mud areas of Iceland*

Fig. 1.31 *Iceland. What are the advantages of using hot springs for heating? How do you think this hot water helps farming and recreation?*

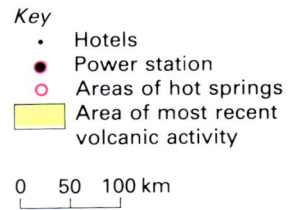

Fig. 1.33 *Part of a tourist brochure*

Only one-sixth of Iceland is habitable which means this is truly one of the few places in the world where you can get away – really away – from the bustle of city life, enjoy nature with no-one around to bother you, and yet still be close to civilisation. The feeling of adventure in Iceland is heightened by magnificent nature where you can observe newly extinct volcanoes side by side with vast icecaps. Hot springs, geysers and lava fields, which only recently were red-hot and glowing in the night, add other dimensions seldom experienced elsewhere.

2 ROCKS AND THE LANDSCAPE

Rocks and landscapes

Rocks differ in their hardness and structure, so they produce contrasting landscapes. There are three broad groups of rocks: igneous, metamorphic and sedimentary.

Igneous rocks

These are produced by volcanic action as molten magma from deep in the Earth forces its way up through the crust. There are two broad types. Some magma cools deep in the crust. This forms intrusive rocks. Other magma reaches the surface as lava or ash and is called extrusive. Intrusive rocks, such as granite, cool more slowly and so contain more crystals. Intrusive rocks produce the hardest type of rock since crystals interlock strongly. Granite is an intrusive rock but comes to the surface when surrounding rocks are worn away. As it reaches the surface it tends to expand and crack, forming joints creating a distinctive landscape.

Fig. 2.2 *Typical granite scenery. How would you describe this landscape?*

Fig. 2.1 *The granite area of Dartmoor*

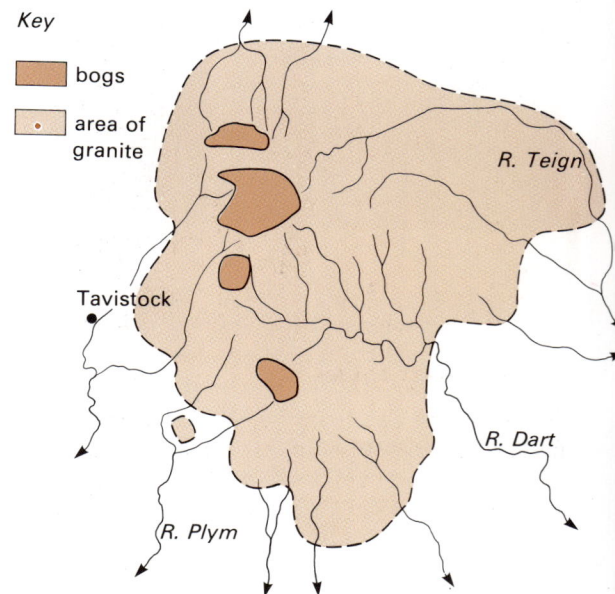

Figure 2.1 shows the granite outcrop that forms the highland area of Dartmoor rising to over 600 m. The rock does not let water through (it is impervious) so there are many rivers, and flatter or hollow areas form extensive bogs. Figure 2.2 is a field sketch of a typical granite scene. The large boulders form a feature called a tor, the exact shape of which is controlled by the pattern of joints.

Metamorphic rocks

These are formed by the heat and pressure of earth movements squashing and altering existing rocks. Slate, for example, is the metamorphic rock produced from mudstone and shale. Metamorphic rocks are hard but they can often be split easily in one direction, as in the case of slate.

Figure 2.3 shows a typical slate landscape in North Wales. Much of the landscape has been altered by human activity. The slate has been quarried and mined for roofing slates and road surfacing.

Fig. 2.3 *Slate scenery, North Wales. Why does the slate form a jagged, angular and high landscape?*

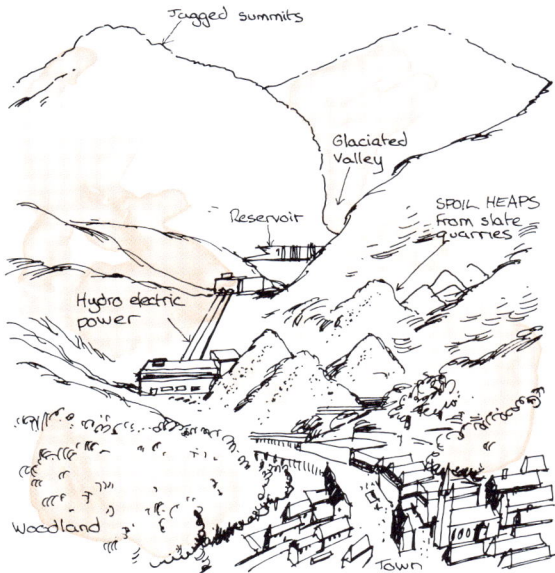

Sedimentary rocks

These are formed from fragments worn away from rocks and then deposited as sediment in lakes, seas and even deserts. The fragments are compressed and 'cemented' together to form rocks as fresh layers are deposited on top. Limestone and sandstone are common sedimentary rock types. Figure 2.4 shows the conditions that produce many of the common types of sedimentary rocks. Coal is formed in tropical swamps. Britain has large areas of coal. What does this tell you about Britain's past climate? Sedimentary rocks are the commonest in England but not in Scotland as Scotland was an area of highland rising above the seas into which the sediment was deposited.

Most sedimentary rocks contain horizontal layers called beds. These beds are formed by slight changes in the conditions of deposition, such as more or less mud being washed into the sea. Only sedimentary rocks contain fossils. Sedimentary rocks vary a great deal in hardness, weaknesses and whether they let water drain through. Therefore they produce varied landscapes, such as the Weald of Kent, shown in figure 2.5.

Fig. 2.4 *Sediments, forming sedimentary rocks. Suggest which types of rocks are formed*

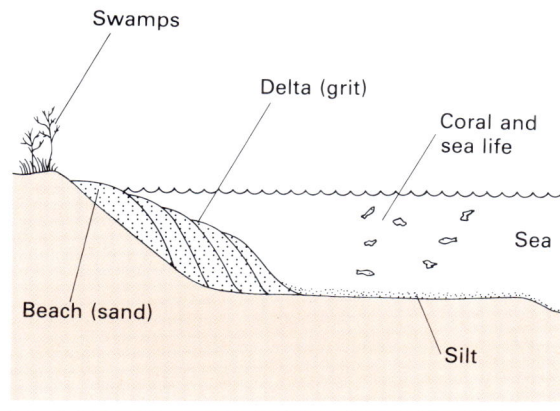

Fig. 2.5 *Part of the Weald of Kent, the South Downs*

Fig. 2.6 *Land use transect*

Chalk		Clay vale	Sandstone
Relief	Scarp slope		
Land use Crops			
Settlement	Nil	Farms	

Activities

1 Complete the transect diagram (fig. 2.6). Try to explain the pattern of relief and land use that you have shown.
2 Why did people in pre-historic times settle on the chalk but not on the clay? Why was the sandstone left wooded but the clay cleared in historic times?

Limestone landscapes

Limestones differ in their hardness and structure depending on the age of their formation. Figure 2.7 shows the two main types in Britain. Carboniferous limestone is 200 million years older than chalk limestone. Which do you think is harder and why? They also differ in their structure. Unlike carboniferous limestone, chalk has no distinctive beds and joints but as it allows water to seep between its rock particles, it is a porous rock. Carboniferous limestone is non-porous but water can seep down through the joint systems.

Joints

Joints are points of weakness that can widen so much that a stream is able to flow down them, as in fig. 2.8 which shows smelt-mill sinks at Malham in the Pennines. Sometimes a very large joint may occur and a hole is produced that is sufficient to swallow an entire river as in the photograph (fig. 2.9).

Fig. 2.9 *Hunt Pot in Ribblesdale, the Pennines. Suggest why chalk rarely has potholes*

Joints also allow erosion and weathering to work on the rock to produce caves, as shown in fig. 2.10. Caves can form along beds, in which case they form horizontal low caves. Inside the limestone caves, dissolved lime is deposited as stalactites as water drips and evaporates from the cave roof, as shown in fig. 2.11. On the cave floor stalagmites form, provided there is no running water to wash away the deposited lime.

Fig. 2.7 *Limestone areas*

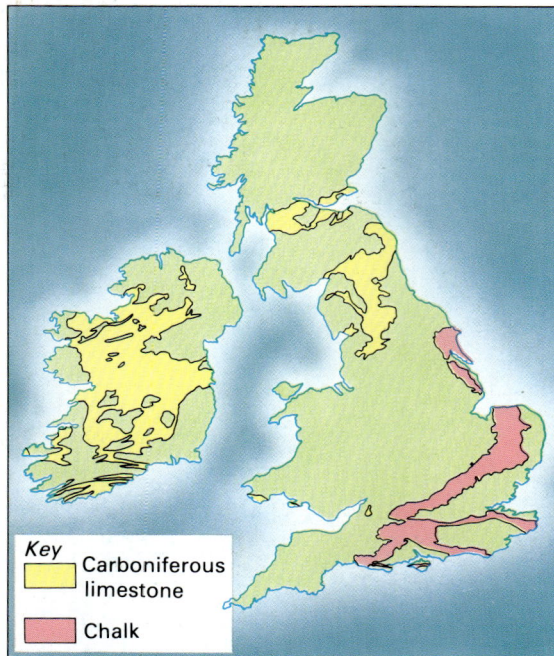

Key
- Carboniferous limestone
- Chalk

Fig. 2.8 *Smelt-mill sinks, Malham Moor*

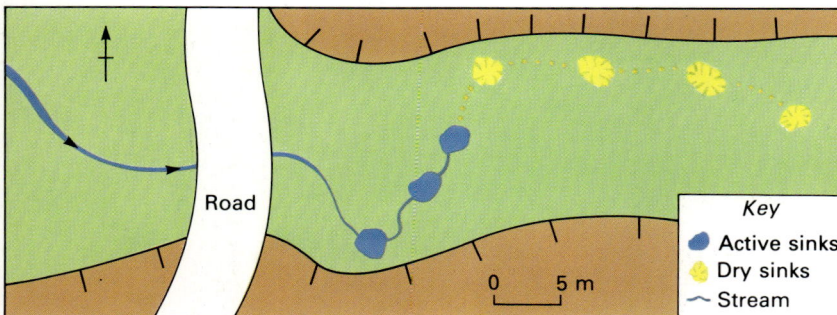

Road

Key
- Active sinks
- Dry sinks
- Stream

0   5 m

Fig. 2.10 *Caves near Settle, the Pennines. Draw a large sketch of this photograph and label the beds and joints. Why do chalk caves rarely exist for long?*

Fig. 2.11 *Stalactites in a cave in the Castleton area of the Peak District*

Limestone pavements

Together the joints and beds form limestone pavements such as that at Malham Cove shown in the photograph (fig. 2.12). The enlarged joints are called grykes and the blocks of limestone left in between are called clints. Carboniferous limestone produces angular steep slopes or scars and piles of coarse debris called scree. Chalk, which lacks beds and joints, produces more smooth, rounded slopes. Why do you think it is so difficult to walk on carboniferous limestone slopes?

Valleys

Both rocks produce dry valleys. The valleys were probably originally cut when water was able to flow over these rocks during the last ice age, when the ground was frozen. Carboniferous limestone may produce steeper-sided valleys or gorges, as in the case of Goredale shown in fig. 2.13. Chalk produces gentler valleys. The water that sinks down the joints or through the porous chalk eventually reappears as springs.

Fig. 2.12 *Limestone pavement above Malham Cove*

Fig. 2.13 *Goredale, looking south. How do you think this gorge was formed? Can you suggest why the volume of the river is steadily decreasing?*

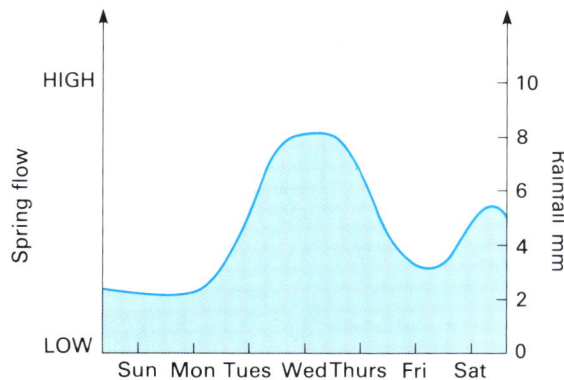

Fig. 2.14 *Spring flow and rainfall for a week in March*

Rainfall
Sun. – 10 mm
Mon. – 9 mm
Tues. – 0 mm
Wed. – 0 mm
Thurs. – 6 mm
Fri. – 2 mm
Sat. – 0 mm

Activities

1 Study fig. 2.14. Copy out the graph of spring flow and use the rainfall figures to add a graph for rainfall. Try to explain the difference in the pattern.
2 Design an experiment to measure the flow of a spring. How would you trace the origin of the spring water?
3 Make a list of place names ending in the word 'bourne'. Can you discover what a bourne is? It appears in many chalk place names.

The uses of rocks

Quarrying

Limestone is quarried for building stone as shown in the photograph of the Winspit quarry, in Dorset (fig. 2.15). Both chalk and other limestones are quarried, crushed, roasted and turned into hydrated lime. Some of this is used to add lime to acid soils to help farming and some is used to make cement. Some is even used in talcum powder. Look at fig. 2.16 of part of Wharfedale in the Pennines. The quarry at Cracoe alone produces 1 million tonnes a year. This helps provide jobs, keeps a rail link open and has helped improve local roads, but quarries can also create problems as they are very dangerous and unattractive.

Fig. 2.15 *Limestone quarry. How does the structure of the rock aid the quarryworkers?*

Mining

Limestone may contain important mineral veins. There are over sixty old lead-mining shafts on Grassington Moor. These became disused in the late nineteenth century as the price of lead fell and as flooding caused more and more problems. The photograph (fig. 2.17) shows the typical remains of one of the old smelt mills.

Tourism

Much of the Yorkshire Dales National Park is on limestone. Many tourists visit this area to see the harsh limestone scenery, waterfalls and other attractions, as shown in the Wharfedale area diagram (fig. 2.16).

Fig. 2.16 *Part of Wharfedale in the Pennines. What problems can quarries create? What would you do with the old quarries?*

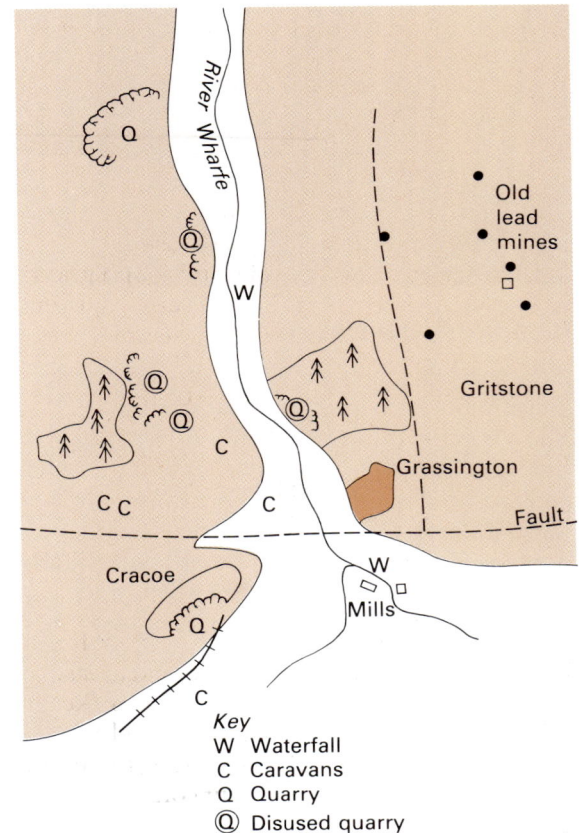

Key
W Waterfall
C Caravans
Q Quarry
ⓠ Disused quarry

Fig. 2.17 *Smelt mill on Malham Moor. Why might these remains prove to be a problem to farmers?*

Activities

The table below shows the result of a field survey of the number of visitors entering Malham village over the period of a week in early summer.

Sun	Mon	Tues	Wed	Thur	Fri	Sat
2021	212	80	340	312	917	1814

1 Draw a graph or chart of these figures. Why does the number of visitors vary over the week?
2 Can you suggest why this area becomes so congested at weekends in August? Imagine you live in the village of Malham. Suggest two differing attitudes and reactions to this stream of visitors.

Farming

Limestone areas have long been used for sheep farming. The dry soils and tough grass have suited sheep, and they can also cope with the more exposed climate on these uplands. Today the use of fertilisers has allowed much of the lower chalk downland to be ploughed up and used for cereal growing. Why do you think that the EEC encouraged this trend? In the upland areas beef cattle are being introduced to lower slopes.

Forestry

Some attempts have been made to plant lines of trees on the scree slopes of upland areas. Trees have been planted across valleys like Wharfedale to act as windbreaks to help farming. Forestry has not been very successful as soils high in lime do not suit conifer plantations which prefer acid soils.

Water supply

Chalk is a porous rock and so is ideal for water storage. London traditionally relied on the chalk of the Thames basin to supply a large proportion of its water needs. Figure 2.18 shows the chalk basin under London. If a well is bored at A then the water will flow out under its own pressure. This is called artesian water and much of it has been stored in the porous chalk for thousands of years. Today the pumping of this water has had to be reduced to conserve it and prevent the land above from sinking. This sinking had caused a potential problem of flooding. The minerals dissolved in the water may aid health. Many limestone springs, such as that in fig. 2.19, are used for local water supplies and may have led to villages growing up around them.

Fig. 2.18 *The Thames basin's acquifer*

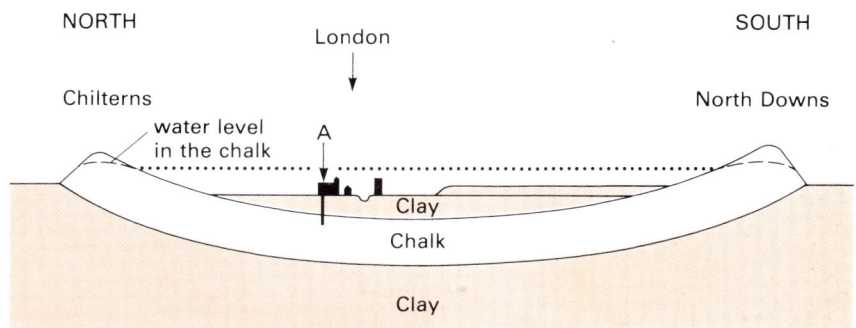

Fig. 2.19 *Spring in Crummackdale, Pennines, where pervious limestone overlays impervious slates*

Other uses

Much of the Salisbury Plain area of Wiltshire is a military range for the army and a weapons test site. Can you discover what happened to the village of Imber in the area?

Economic activities

Damaging the environment

In the 1980s Tarmac Roadstone tried to extend their quarry at Topley Pike in the Peak District National Park. The proposal was to extend the quarry from 31 ha to 38.7 ha and so gain an extra 7.7 million tonnes in extractable limestone.

On 22 May 1986 the Government dismissed the appeal as it was considered that the 'proposed extension would have a major and noticeably adverse impact upon local scenery' which was not offset by the need for the mineral.

Improving the environment

In July 1967 the Cotswold Water Park was designated. The water park extends over 5700 ha in two sections as shown in fig. 2.20. It is an area of old and active gravel workings dating from the 1920s. The area lacks good landscape features other than the artificial lakes formed in old gravel workings. There are over fifty lakes, many of which have been leased by the companies to recreational clubs and others have been left as nature reserves. The attraction of the water park will grow as the gravel companies excavate larger lakes over the next ten years. The table (fig. 2.22) shows the use of these lakes.

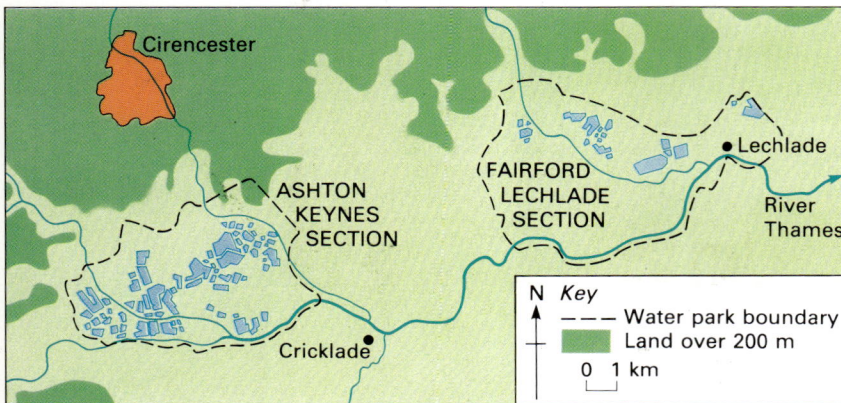

Fig. 2.20 *Cotswold Water Park. Why might some of these areas be dangerous to unwary walkers?*

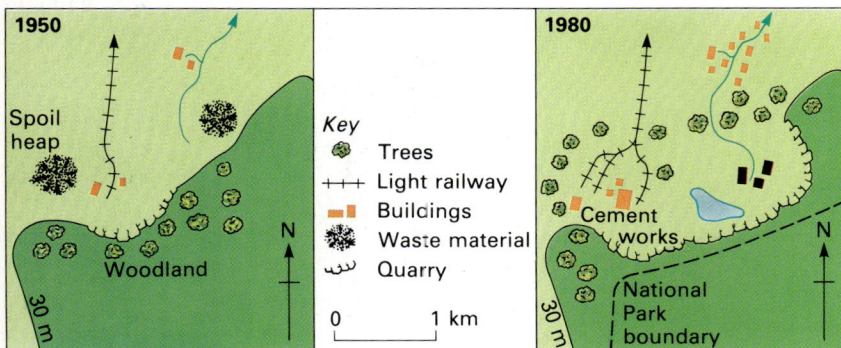

Fig. 2.21 *Changes at a quarry 1950 to 1980*

Fig. 2.22 *Uses of the lakes in the Cotswold Water Park 1986. Draw a graph to show the importance of the various uses. Why is fishing more common than power-boat racing.*

| | Number of lakes | | |
Activity	Ashton Keynes /South Cerney	Fairford	Area (ha)
Coarse fishing	16	7	214
Game fishing	5	3	35
Dinghy sailing	5	3	192
Board sailing	3	—	40
Canoeing	1	—	17
Rowing	1	—	30
Power-boat racing	—	1	11
Water skiing	2	2	73
Multiple use	4	2	160
Total	37	18	772

Activities

Look at fig. 2.21 which shows changes at a quarry.
1 What changes were made between 1950 and 1980? Distinguish between beneficial and harmful changes caused by the development of the quarry.
2 Why might a local conservationist disagree with a local villager about the planned extension? What arguments and attitudes would each produce to support their views?

Preserving the environment

In 1906 the Grand Canyon Game reserve was established in Arizona to protect game animals from being hunted and the area was declared a national monument in 1908 to stop the threat of mining claims in the canyon. In 1919 it became a national park and was extended in 1975 to include Marble Canyon and part of the Lake Mead recreation area, as shown in fig. 2.24. It was vital to preserve this 443 km long canyon that plunges in depth to over 1.5 km as it gives a unique 2000 million years' geological record and contains six major biotic communities. The canyon itself has long acted as a geographical barrier which has led to the isolation of the animals and so created a unique variety of wildlife. This area has to be protected and preserved as it is so unique, as the photograph (fig. 2.23) shows. Facilities are very limited in the park and are kept to a few sites. In 1972 even boat trips were limited to minimise damage to the environment. Much is done to educate visitors, and nature trails and hiking trails help maximise interaction with the environment but minimise damage. In 1963 the Glen Canyon Dam was built upstream from the park.

What effect do you think this might have on the canyon? Why might a developing country find it harder to justify such conservation schemes?

Fig. 2.23 *The Grand Canyon. What damage might still occur to the area?*

Fig. 2.24 *Grand Canyon National Park*

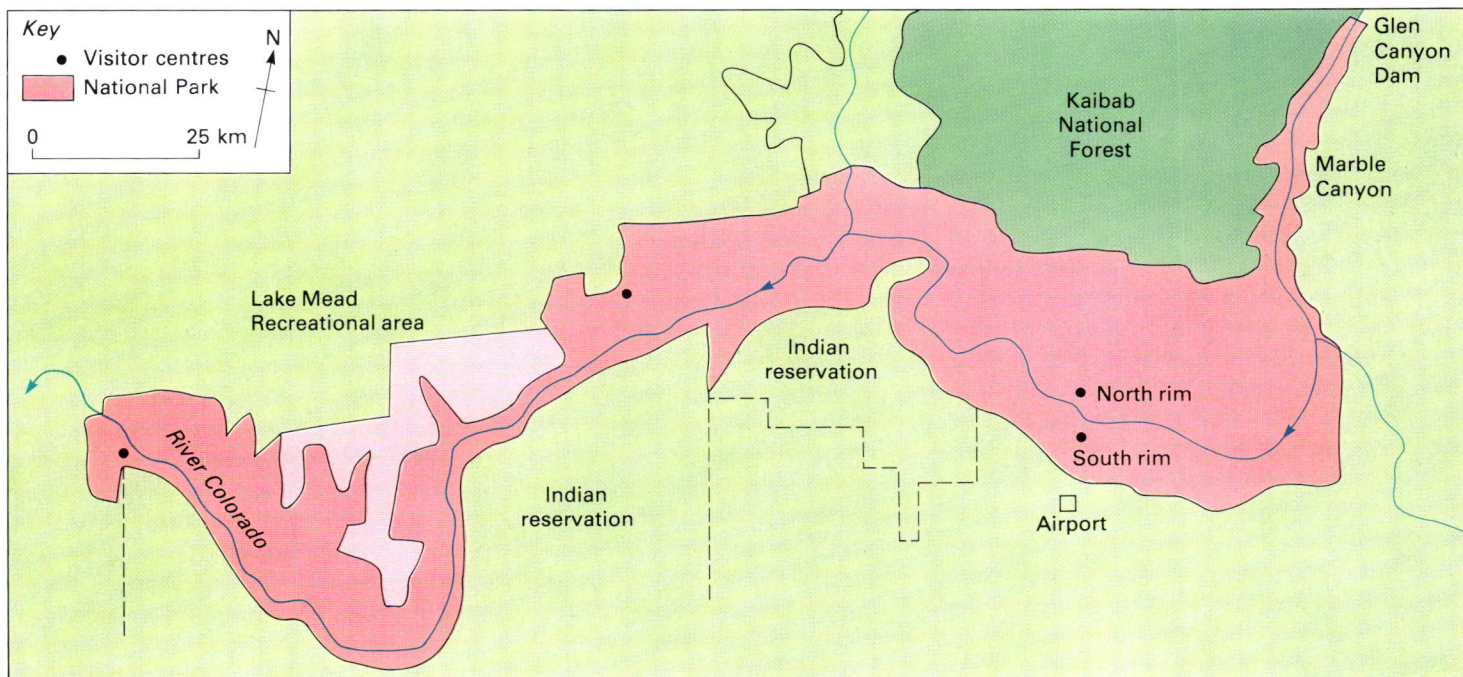

Key
• Visitor centres
National Park
0   25 km
N

Glen Canyon Dam
Kaibab National Forest
Marble Canyon
Lake Mead Recreational area
Indian reservation
North rim
South rim
Airport
Indian reservation
River Colorado

3 WEATHER VARIATIONS, HAZARDS AND IMPACTS

Measuring weather

Weather can be described as the day-to-day conditions in the atmosphere. A number of these conditions are measured at regular intervals at meteorological stations, as shown in fig. 3.1. This field sketch was drawn near the harbour-master station at Milford Haven, an oil port in South Wales. Why does a harbour-master need meteorological information?

Precipitation

This includes rain, snow, hail and dew. It is measured once a day using a rain gauge, as shown in fig. 3.2.

Care must be taken to select a suitable site for gauges to ensure accurate rainfall readings.

Fig. 3.1 *Typical meteorological station*

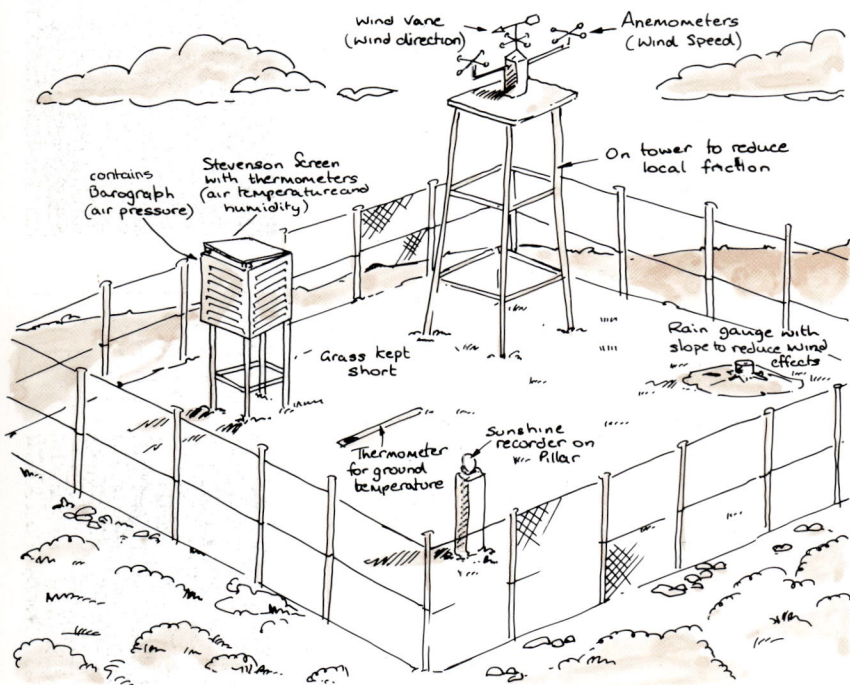

Fig. 3.2 *Rain gauge*

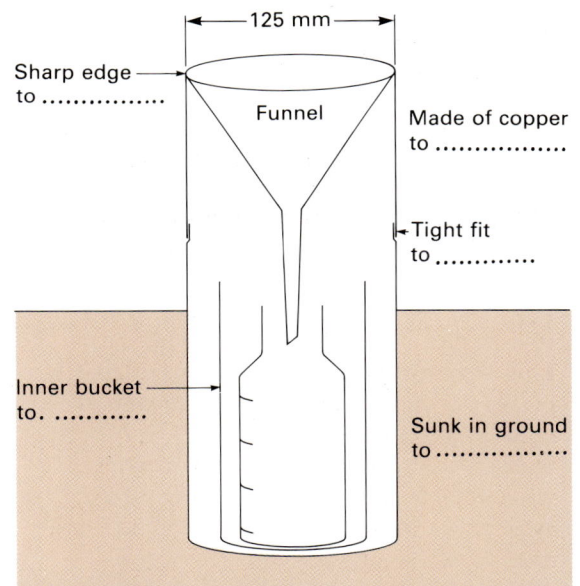

Activities

1 Copy out the diagram in fig. 3.2 and complete the labels. Why is it partly sunk into the ground?
2 How would you measure snowfall in a gauge?
3 Look at fig. 3.3 and explain why each of the sites (A, B, C and D) is, or is not, suitable as a site for a rain gauge.

Fig. 3.3 *Possible sites for rain gauges*

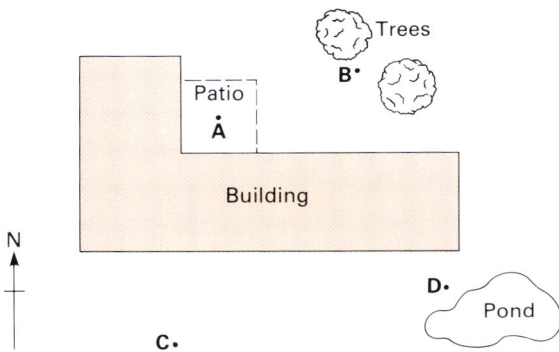

Temperature

This is measured using a thermometer. The most common type used is a maximum and minimum thermometer, as shown in fig. 3.4. As the temperature rises the alcohol expands in the left-hand bulb and it pushes up the index in the right-hand tube. The index is held in place by a tiny brake until it is drawn back and reset by using a magnet. As temperatures fall, the compressed vacuum in the right-hand bulb pushes the alcohol back up the left-hand tube. Again an index is pushed up. This shows the minimum temperature.

This thermometer (or sometimes two separate ones are used) is kept in a Stevenson's screen. This white slatted box is designed to make sure only air-shade temperatures are measured. Figure 3.5 shows a Stevenson screen and the design features needed to keep out direct sunlight.

Wind speed

This is measured with an anemometer. The photograph (fig. 3.6) shows a hand-held version. As the wind blows the 'cups' are blown round, pushing the scale up to show wind speed. How is wind direction measured? Who do you think needs to know the wind speed and direction?

Atmospheric pressure

This is measured using a barometer. There are several kinds of barometer but one of the most useful is a barograph. The photograph (fig. 3.7) shows a barograph. The silver cylinder contains a vacuum. As air pressure increases, the cylinder is compressed. Any movement of the cylinder works a series of levers that operate an ink pen which draws on a slowly rotating drum. The drum rotates once a week and has a section of graph paper fixed to it to take the recording. The instrument has to be adjusted to allow for height above sea-level.

Visibility

Visibility is measured by looking at various landmarks, such as churches, at known distances. If visibility is less than 1000 m the weather condition is called fog. How do you think visibility is measured at night?

Humidity

Humidity is measured using two thermometers, one of which is kept wet. The difference between the two temperatures tells us the dryness of the air. The greater the difference the drier the air! What other methods can be used to measure humidity?

Fig. 3.5 *A Stevenson screen. Copy out the diagram and complete the labels?*

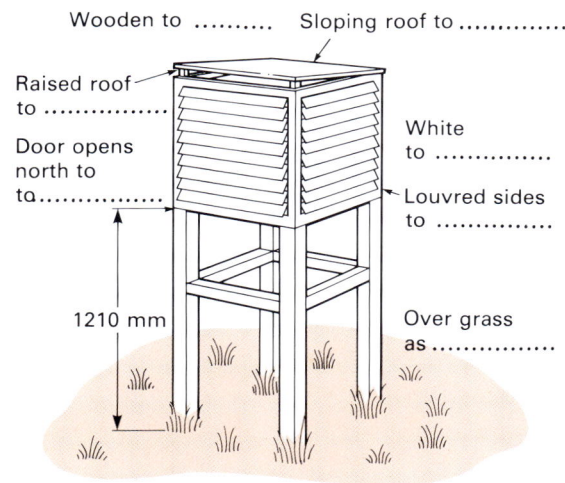

Fig. 3.7 *A barograph. It is usually kept in a glass fronted box to keep out dust and wind. What other types of barometer can you find?*

Fig. 3.4 *Maximum and minimum thermometer. The silver thread in the thermometer is mercury.*

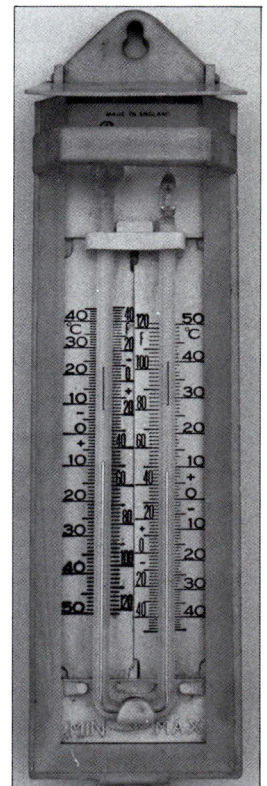

Fig. 3.6 *A hand-held anemometer. It can show the wind speed directly or on the Beaufort scale.*

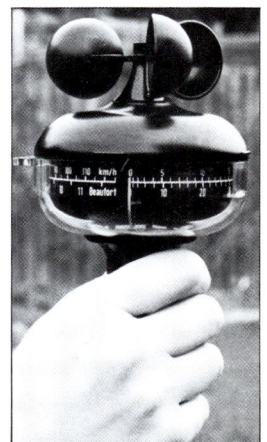

Presenting weather data

Weather recordings are presented in a number of different ways.

Fig. 3.8 *January averages*

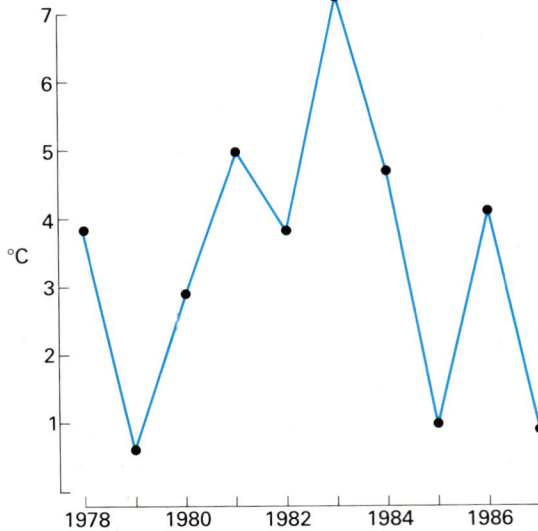

Line graphs

Line graphs are used to show changes that are continuous. A line graph implies that one value changes smoothly to the next with no abrupt break. Such graphs are used to show temperatures over a period of time (fig. 3.8).

Bar charts

These are chiefly used for rainfall figures like those in fig. 3.9, which shows the monthly rainfall totals for an area in northern Nigeria. Such a pattern can cause major problems for human activities such as farming, water supply and river transport.

Fig. 3.9 *Rainfall in northern Nigeria. Why would average monthly rainfall be misleading in an area like this? Why is a bar chart more suitable for showing rainfall than a line graph?*

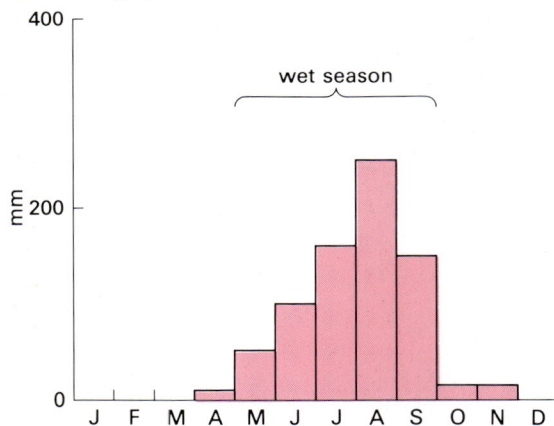

Fig. 3.10 *January temperatures*

	Mean Max	Mean Min	Mean (average)
1978	6.0	1.5	3.8
1979	2.8	−1.6	0.6
1980	5.3	0.6	2.9
1981	7.3	2.6	5.0
1982	6.6	1.1	3.8
1983	9.5	5.1	7.3
1984	7.2	2.1	4.7
1985	3.2	−1.3	1.0
1986	6.5	1.7	4.1
1987	2.7	−1.0	0.9

Activities

Table 3.10 shows temperature figures for an area in January.
1 Work out the overall average for the month of January.
2 Copy out the line graph (fig. 3.8) and add on a line to show the average you worked out. What does this tell you about the usefulness of averages?
3 If the lowest temperature figure is taken from the highest this gives the temperature range. What is the temperature range in this example? Why is the temperature range so low on the equator?

Wind roses

These show both the direction and strength of the wind. Look at fig. 3.11. The wind direction is shown by the direction of the bar and the strength is shown by its width. The frequency of that speed and direction is shown by the length of the bar.

Fig. 3.11 *Wind directions at St Ann's Head, Pembrokeshire. Which is the most common direction of wind shown? Why is a speed over Force 12 so dangerous?*

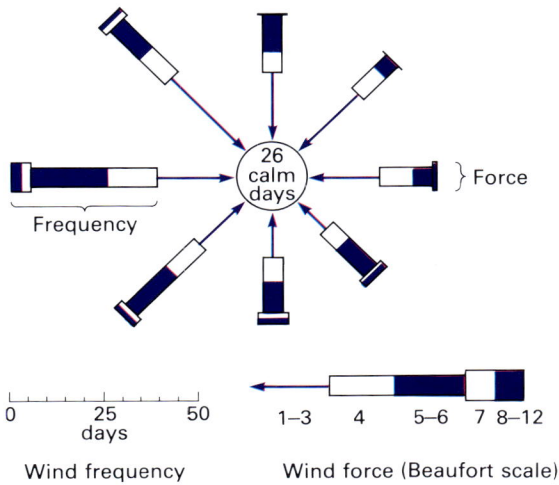

Isolines (isopleths)

Isolines are lines joining points of equal value and so they convert measurements taken at a variety of points into patterns. Other values are estimated. For example it would be assumed that a value of 20 would occur midway between a value of 10 and a value of 30. Isotherms are isolines which join places of equal temperature (fig. 3.12) and isobars join places of equal atmospheric pressure. Isohyets join places of equal rainfall.

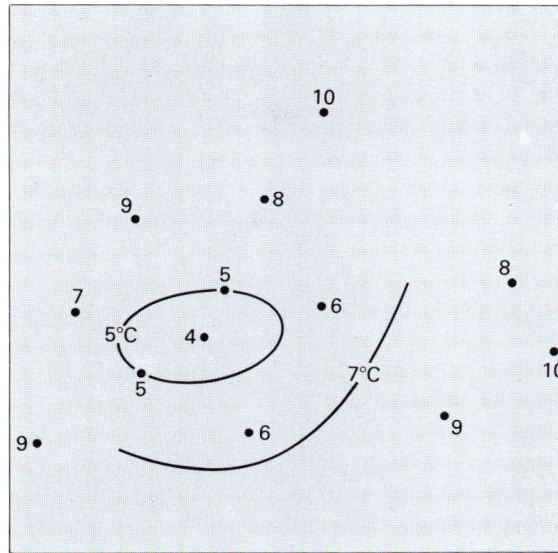

Fig. 3.12 *Isotherm map. Try to complete the isotherms at 2°C intervals. Why might these maps not be totally accurate?*

Weather maps

Weather maps may be very detailed with all the weather recorded at each observation station being shown. Figure 3.13 shows the main symbols used and part of a typical weather map.

Fig. 3.13 *A weather map and weather symbols*

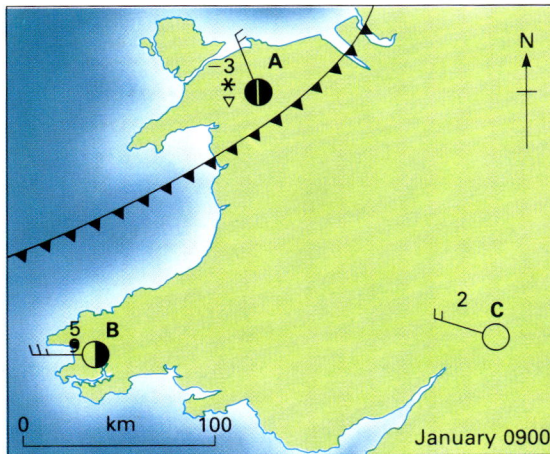

Cloud cover
oktas

0 5
1 6
2 7
3 8
4 Sky obscured (e.g. by fog)

Weather
• rain
9 drizzle
* snow
△ hail
▽ shower
= mist
≡ fog
R̷ thunderstorm
▲▲▲ cold front
●●● warm front
▲●▲ occluded front

Wind direction
knots
Northerly   Easterly

Wind speed
◎ calm
1–2kts
3–7kts
8–12kts
13–17kts
18–22kts
each adds 5kts ± 2
up to 48–52kts

Activities

1 What are the conditions shown at station A and at station B (fig. 3.13)? Suggest why they might be different.
2 Why do the television weather maps use more simple symbols?
3 If the wind at C is 18–22 knots or 37 km/hour, can you forecast the weather at C in ten hours' time? What reduces the accuracy of your forecast?
4 Draw the weather symbols for a station with (a) 3°C, sky obscured by fog, no wind; and (b) 12°C, 7 oktas (eighths) cloud, wind 28–32 knots from SE, thunderstorm.

Weather variations over space

These may be very local, regional or on a continental or world scale. Certain factors, however, tend to explain variations in weather between one place and another.

Latitude

The equator is hotter than the poles. This is due to the curvature of the Earth's surface. Figure 3.14 shows that the Sun's rays have to heat a greater surface (a) at the poles. The rays have also passed through more atmosphere (x) at the poles, so more heat is lost to gases and to dust and is reflected off clouds. Temperatures tend to decrease with distance, both north and south, from the equator. How does this influence the rate of evaporation and the type and amount of precipitation?

Fig. 3.14 *The effect of the Earth's curvature*

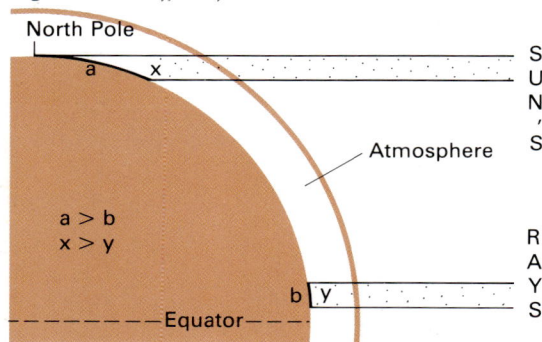

Cold air creates high-pressure areas as the air sinks, and warm air creates low-pressure areas as warm air rises. Wind blows from high to low pressure. This helps explain the world pattern of wind belts shown in fig. 3.15. The wind pattern is not a simple north or south movement as the rotation of the Earth tends to deflect winds to the right in the northern hemisphere and to the left in the southern hemisphere.

Distance from the sea

The sea takes much longer to heat up and to cool down than the land as it takes longer to heat to a greater depth. This is because water is less dense than land, and also it is in constant motion. As it is slow to heat up, the sea remains cool in summer compared to the land. But because it is slow to cool down, in winter the sea is warmer than the land.

Fig. 3.15 *The World's wind system*

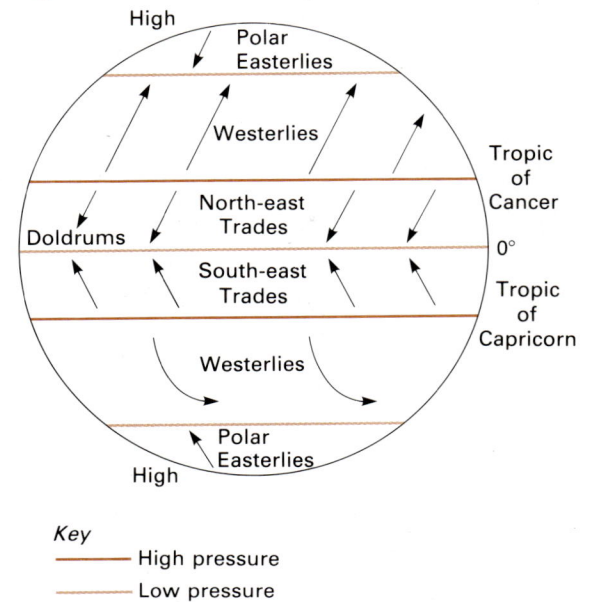

Key
High pressure
Low pressure

Fig. 3.16 *July temperatures for the British Isles*

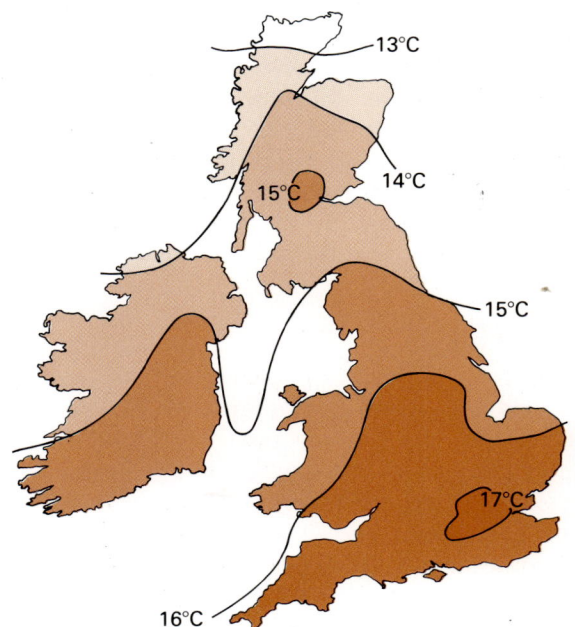

Fig. 3.17 *January temperatures for the British Isles*

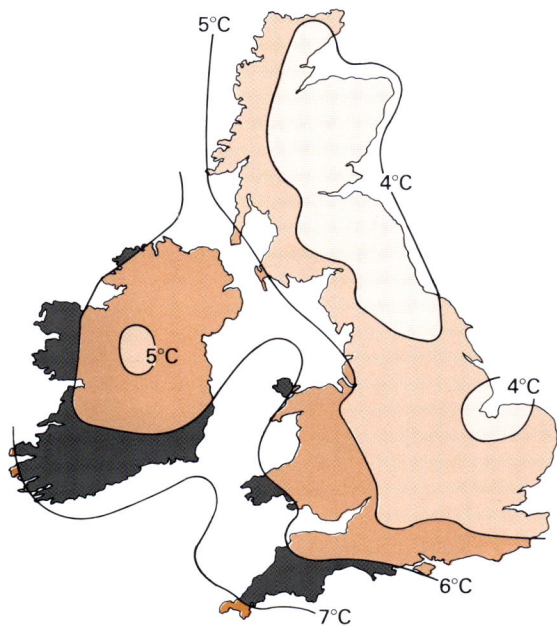

Activities

Look at the map (fig. 3.16).
1 What are the general directions of the isotherms? Where is it coldest?
2 Suggest why the west coast is cooler than the east?
3 Why do you think that London is the hottest area? How do you think that this affects the pattern of rainfall?
4 Look at the map (fig. 3.17). Make a list of the ways this map differs from fig. 3.16? Where is it hottest now?
5 Suggest why there is a difference between the north and south coasts?
6 In what ways is the shape of the coastline important in controlling the sea's influence?

Fig. 3.18 *Annual rainfall and main air masses for the British Isles. Where is it wettest? Where is it driest? How does this pattern reflect the relief of the land? Why does Polar Maritime air bring more rain than Polar Continental? Which air mass does the British Isles get most often?*

Relief of the land

Temperatures decrease with height, partly because with higher altitudes the air is thinner and it is windier. Relief also has a large impact on precipitation. Steep high relief forces air to rise and form clouds. These may bring rain to slopes facing the wind. Look at the map (fig. 3.18) which shows the rainfall pattern for the British Isles. Relief also affects the type of precipitation. The Welsh Mountains have an average of twenty more days of snow each year than flat East Anglia. Relief will also influence both wind speed and wind direction.

Wind direction

Winds tend to bring air from other areas. These air masses bring different conditions, which depend upon the area that the air has come from. Figure 3.18 also shows the common air-mass types that reach the British Isles. Tropical Maritime air is warm and wet as it comes from the Atlantic in tropical areas. Polar Continental air is cold and dry as it comes from Siberia in winter.

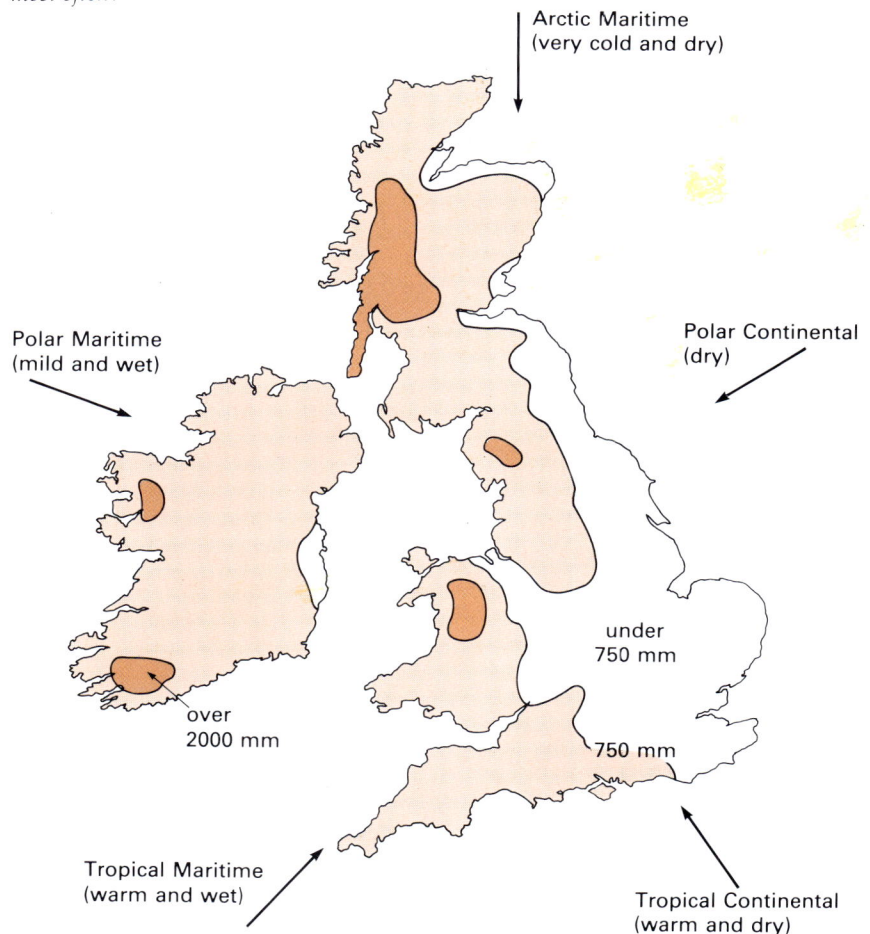

Weather variations over time

Weather conditions may change each minute but it is more usual to study them over a day, a month or a year. Sometimes even longer periods are needed to see patterns in weather. For short-term forecasts of a few days, weathermen or meteorologists use satellites to see weather systems many miles away. (Balloons and weather ships were used before satellites were invented.) These weather systems are usually different pressure systems and they bring distinct changes in weather over time.

Fig. 3.19 *Valley fog in Switzerland*

High pressure (anticyclone)

Anticyclones persist for many days. Within them air sinks which maintains high pressure. This means that little air can rise up to form clouds. Cloudless skies are typical of anticyclones. The cloudless skies produce hot sunny days but radiation (heat loss) at night causes the nights to be cold. In summer, anticyclones often end in thunderstorms as the ground becomes hot enough to send air up, overcoming the pattern of sinking air, which forms clouds as in fig. 3.20.

Fig. 3.20 *Anticyclone – Southampton. What evidence can you see that this photograph was taken in summer?*

In winter the clear skies at night lead to frost or fog being formed as the air remains calm. This is shown in the photograph (fig. 3.19). Frost and fog are most likely to form in moist low-lying areas. Both can be very hazardous especially to road traffic. Sections of the southern part of the M25 are prone to fog in anticyclones. Anticyclones, with their clear skies, may bring long periods without rain. This happened in England and Wales in the drought of 1976.

Fig. 3.21 *Winter anticyclone over north-west Europe*

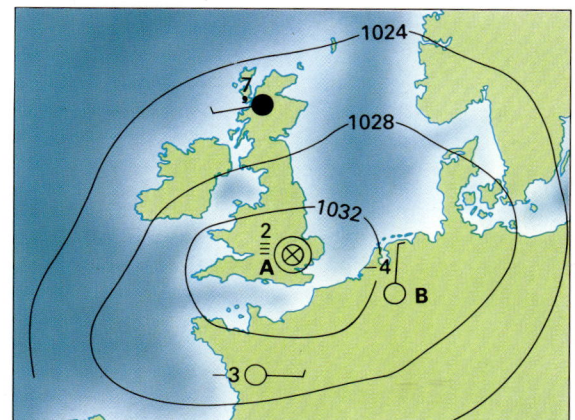

Activities

The map (fig. 3.21) shows an anticyclone over Europe in winter.
1 Use the weather symbols chart on page 23 (fig. 3.13) to say what the weather is at weather stations A and B.
2 In what ways does the weather differ at the two stations? Explain these differences.

Low pressure (depression)

These form where warm and cold air meet along the polar front. The cold air is heavier and denser so undercuts the lighter warmer air forcing it to rise. This creates low pressure. The map (fig. 3.22) shows a depression over the British Isles.

The warm front is where warm air slides over cold air but at the cold front, cold air undercuts the warm air forcing it to rise sharply. This uplift causes the air to cool, condense and form clouds. So depressions tend to bring rain. The thick cloud at the front reduces the sunshine hours in a depression. Can you find out how a tropical depression or hurricane differs from a temperate depression?

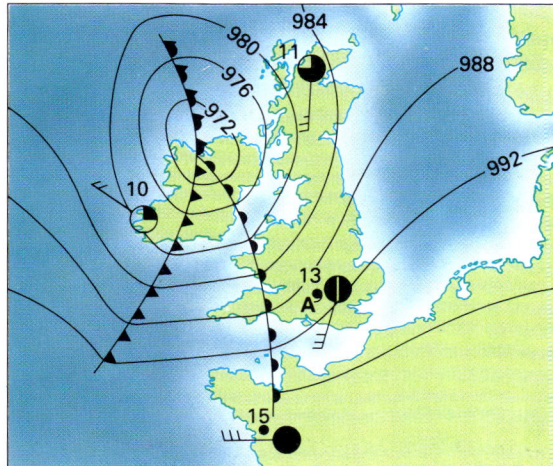

Fig. 3.22 *Depression over the British Isles. What differences are there compared to an anticyclone? What is the weather now like at A?*

Fig. 3.23 *Weather cross section of a depression*

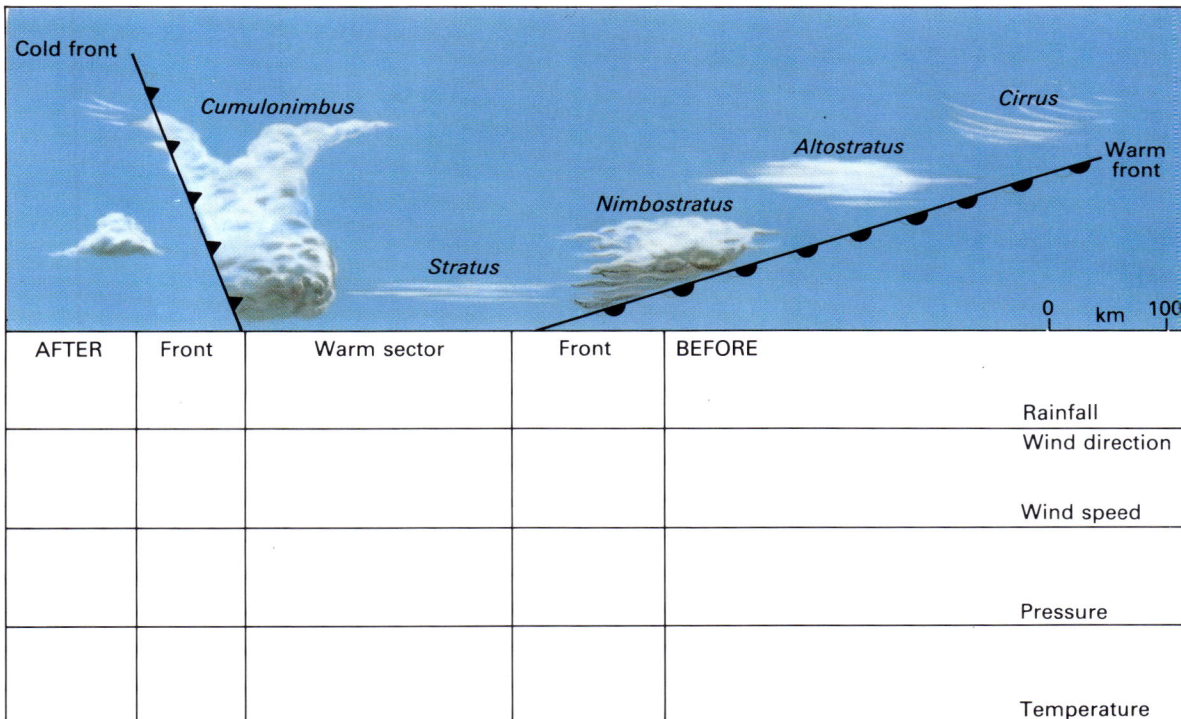

AFTER	Front	Warm sector	Front	BEFORE	
					Rainfall
					Wind direction
					Wind speed
					Pressure
					Temperature

Activities

1 Look at the map (fig. 3.22). Use the information and the section through the depression shown in fig. 3.23 to complete the rest of the table of weather conditions.
2 How would you be able to tell if a depression was approaching? Why is there a gap in the rain in the warm sector?
3 Keep a record of wet days for a term. How many of these are caused by the passage of a depression?

Human influence on weather

Locally

People may create small-scale differences in climate (called microclimate) by removing or planting vegetation, by putting up buildings and by creating bodies of water. Sometimes the effect is direct, as when a power station creates clouds due to the heat and moisture from its chimney. The map (fig. 3.24) shows a local field survey. The building causes wind speeds and directions to vary greatly. The building may store heat and remain warm even in the late afternoon.

Fig. 3.24 *Temperature pattern, December, 10 am. Why does the weather vary around the building?*

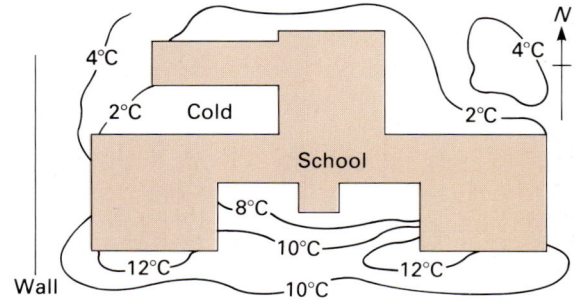

Activities

The table (fig. 3.25) shows rainfall under two different trees measured in December.
1 Draw a graph to show the differences between the two measurements. Explain the contrast.
2 How would the two trees differ in the ways that they influence wind speed and evaporation?
3 Try to measure the difference in temperature between a grassed and a concrete surface. Why might they differ?

Fig. 3.25 *Rainfall in millimetres. The dotted line represents the trunk of the tree.*

			Deciduous tree					
W E S T	41	35	30	17	13	32	35	36 E A S T
			Conifer					
W E S T	35	18	12	6	5	10	15	20 E A S T
			Distance from the tree					
	2m	1.5	1	.5	0	.5	1	1.5	2m

Regionally

Human activity can alter or exaggerate a weather feature. The map (fig. 3.26) shows north-east Brazil. This area has anticyclones for at least six months each year so drought is common but human activity has extended this drought, mainly by careless farming. Much of

Fig. 3.26 *Drought area of north-east Brazil*

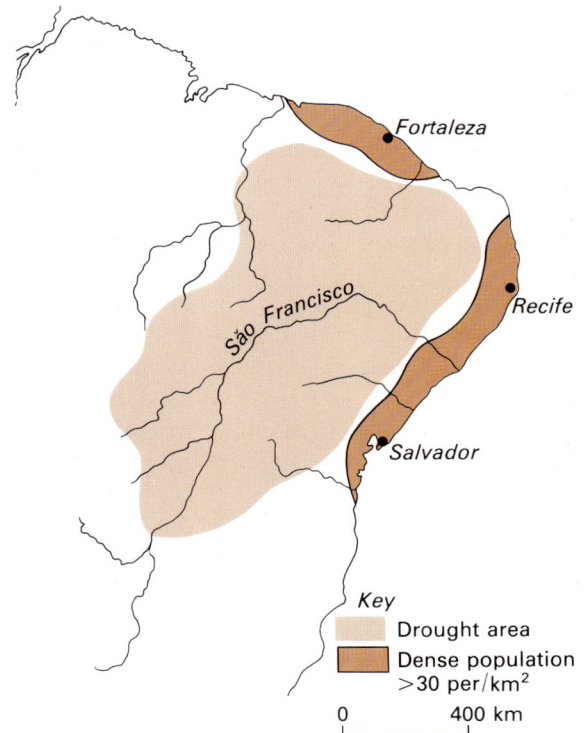

Key
Drought area
Dense population >30 per/km²

0   400 km

this area is the scrub forest of Caatinga, and it was used for extensive cattle and sheep farming. Overgrazing can produce both drought and floods, as shown in fig. 3.27. It is very difficult to break such a vicious circle. People make the problem worse by cutting down the trees for fuel and for new farmland. This removes an important source of water vapour. In 1959 a regional development agency in Brazil was set up to increase food production, diversify the local economy and shift vulnerable population into other areas. How would each of these approaches help? Who might object to such a policy and why? More recently there has been a policy of building wells and reservoirs which may alter the rainfall as well as supply water. In some cases, as in Australia, clouds have been seeded with silver iodide to cause condensation and precipitation. Why would this be of little use in north-east Brazil?

Also large urban areas may have an impact on the weather of a region. London, for example, acts as a 'heat island' because the buildings absorb heat during the day and because urban factors like traffic, factories and people produce heat. Figure 3.28 shows the contrast between central London and the outer suburbs.

Globally

The world's weather is increasingly influenced by human activities. Car exhaust fumes and industrial air pollution threaten to raise the carbon dioxide content of the air producing a 'greenhouse effect' that could raise world temperatures by 2–3°C over the next fifty years. This could lead to a major rise in sea-level as the ice caps melt. Extensive removal of the world's forests (40 ha of tropical rainforest is being cleared every minute) may further increase carbon dioxide in the air as much of it is burned and forests are major absorbers of carbon dioxide from the air. Also it brings a decrease in rainfall which may lead to the extension of deserts causing a major shift in the world's weather patterns. The increasing number of tropical hurricanes and regional droughts may be the first signs of this shift.

Fig. 3.27 The effects of overgrazing

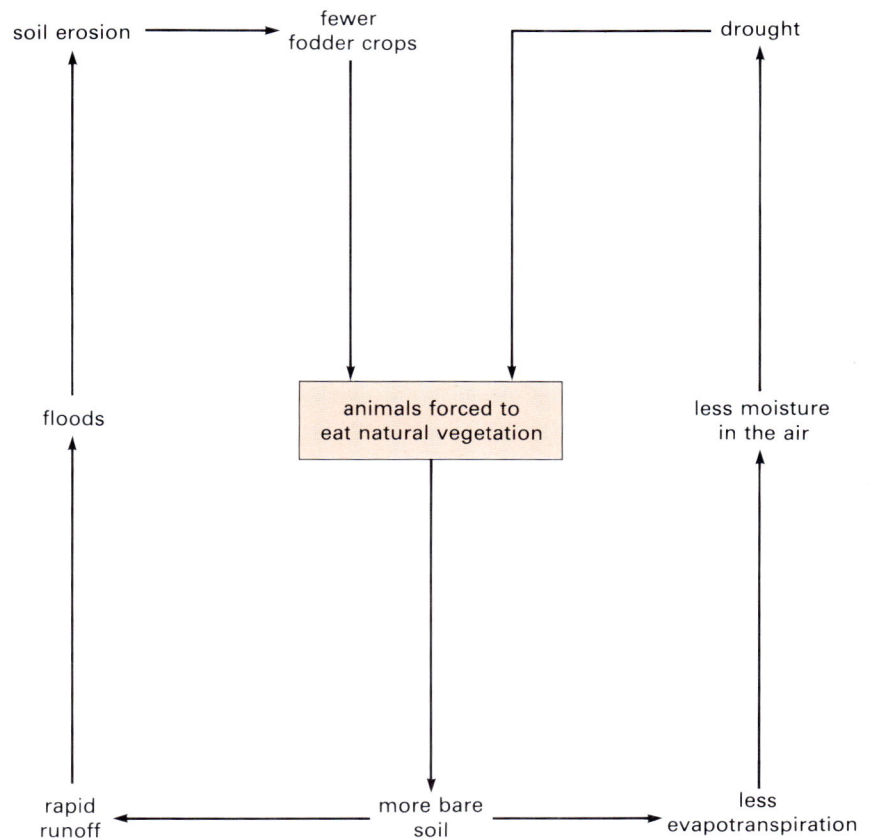

Fig. 3.28 The microclimate of London. Why might the temperature contrast be different for central London and the suburbs between the day and the night?

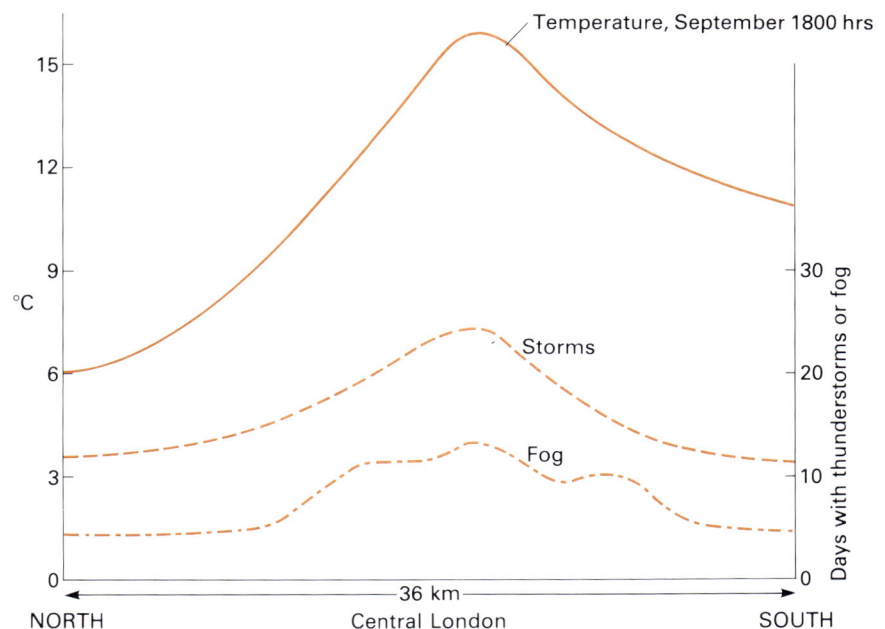

Weather hazards

Extreme forms of weather can cause great damage and even death, usually because they are unexpected.

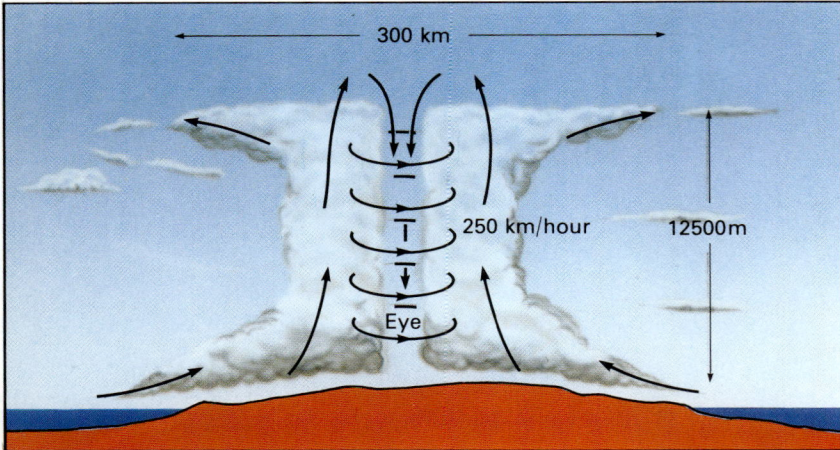

Fig. 3.29 *A cross section of a hurricane*

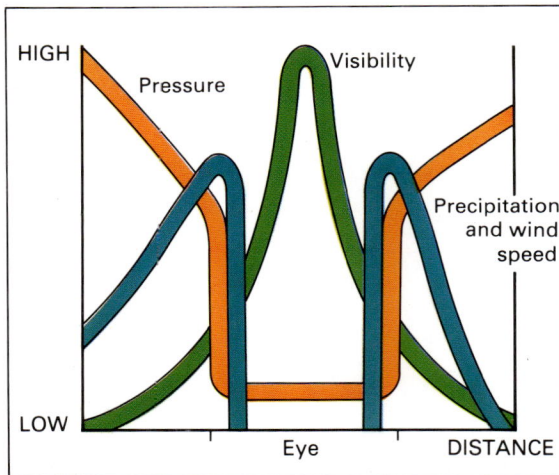

Fig. 3.30 *Weather in a hurricane. Why might the eye itself be a hazard to people?*

Winds

These include tornadoes, which are intense funnels of wind rarely more than 600 m wide and which contain vertical winds that can reach 400 km/hour. The great difference in pressure between the funnel and its central 'vacuum' can cause buildings to explode and debris to be lifted up many metres. Tornadoes occur during summer thunderstorms in areas such as the Middle West of the USA where they do great damage.

The greatest wind hazard is the hurricane. These are intense tropical storms that develop over the warm tropical seas and then swing across tropical land masses causing devastation. Look at fig. 3.29 and at the graph (fig. 3.30). Rainfall may exceed 2500 mm in

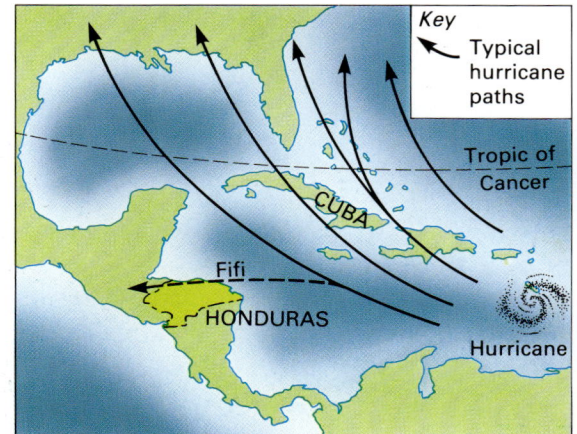

Fig. 3.31 *Hurricane tracks*

Activities

The map (fig. 3.31) shows the typical hurricane paths over the Caribbean. In November 1974, Honduras was hit by Hurricane Fifi which left 8000 dead and the economy wrecked.

1 Why do you think Fifi did so much damage to this poor country? Honduras relied almost totally on exporting bananas. Why was this so risky? Why were the coastal settlements so badly hit?
2 Who should pay for the hurricane damage to countries such as Honduras. Can you explain your answer?
3 Gales in Britain can also do considerable damage. Why are they more common in coastal areas? What activities do you think are worse hit?
4 Imagine that you are in a hurricane. How would you react and what would you do to reduce the damage to your home?

twenty hours. The eye is an area of calm and clear skies formed by descending air. The exact damage done by a hurricane is related to

1 the existence of a storm detection and warning system;
2 the existence of good communications to help warn people;
3 the mobility of the population at risk;
4 the type of building material;
5 the height and relief of the land; and
6 the frequency of hurricanes.

The damage is done by these factors: the high winds that may exceed 300 km/hour in gusts, flooding due to rain and coastal tidal waves caused by the low pressure and strong winds.

Heavy rain

This can produce sudden floods, usually in summer, as shown in this photograph (fig. 3.32) taken in North Wales in August. Sometimes intense thunderstorms can bring 50 mm of rain in an hour and also lightning strikes that may cause fires or damage buildings.

Fig. 3.32 *Floods! Why are these floods more common in summer? Why do farmers fear such summer thunderstorms?*

Hail

This can knock down crops and damage buildings. In 1980 one hailstorm in the Midlands area of Britain cost over £20 million in smashed commercial greenhouses.

Fog

Some areas are very prone to fog (visibility under 1 km). Usually these areas are low lying and near rivers. They occur in calm conditions in anticyclones, often during autumn nights. Fog reduces visibility making sea, road and air travel dangerous. Sometimes industrial fumes or car exhaust gases get mixed into the fog to form smog that may kill the very young and

very old by making breathing difficult. In December 1952 such a smog in London killed 4000. Why is there little risk of this happening in London today, but more risk in the developing countries such as Brazil and India?

Drought

Some areas such as deserts have prolonged droughts while others have seasonal ones. The African Savannah has a seasonal drought of six to eight months, but it is the unexpected drought that is the hazard. In Britain, normally a wet country, there was a drought for sixteen months from 1975 to 1977 with rainfall 40% below average. Figure 3.33 shows the impact of a drought.

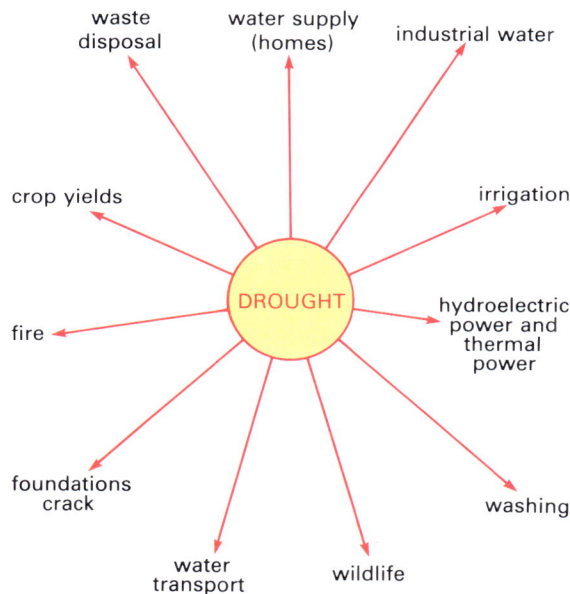

Fig. 3.33 *The impact of drought. How would each of these items be influenced by a lack of water?*

Intense cold

Prolonged 'freeze-ups' and heavy snowfalls can be major hazards. The newspaper article (fig. 3.34) suggests some of the problems faced by the elderly in such a cold spell. Freezing conditions can disrupt transport by freezing diesel oil in lorries and making roads very slippery. Electricity lines and overhead railway power lines may be brought down by the weight of ice or snow. What damage can snow and frost do to homes and to farming? In countries such as Iceland and Finland such conditions are less of a problem because the population expects them every winter and are better prepared.

Fig. 3.34 *Problems for the old*

HELP THE OLD THIS WINTER!

'Help the Aged' ask all people with elderly neighbours to keep a check on them this winter. It is essential that the old keep warm, well fed and mobile to reduce the risk of hypothermia, but unguarded fires can be a major risk to the elderly during the winter. Neighbours should offer to shop for the aged to reduce the risks of old people falling on icy pavements. Many plumbers offer to unfreeze or repair frozen heaters and pipes for pensioners at reduced rates.

The influence of weather

Settlement

People prefer settlement locations with plenty of sunshine and shelter from cold winds and heavy rains. The field sketch (fig. 3.35) shows a typical valley in Switzerland. Settlements are built on sunny south-facing slopes while forest grows on the shaded north-facing slopes.

Fig. 3.35 *A typical Swiss valley showing land use. What hazard might form on the south-facing slopes in early spring?*

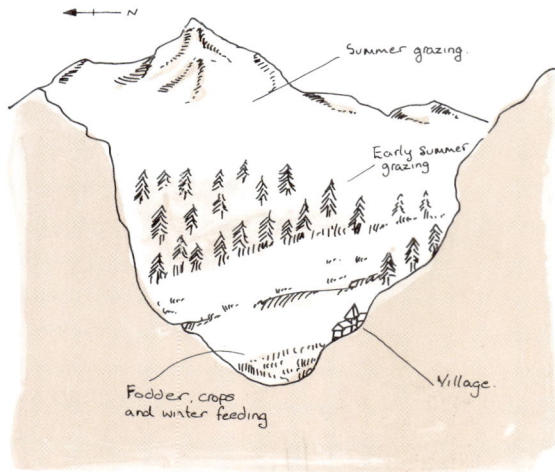

Farming

South-facing slopes get more sun so they tend to be cultivated, unlike north-facing slopes. Cropping patterns change with height of the land as temperature and rainfall alter with altitude. On a larger scale, average weather or climate can have a large impact on farming patterns. Look at the map (fig. 3.37) of the general pattern of British farming. In tropical countries rainfall has a greater impact than temperature differences. Figure 3.36 shows the main types of farming in Nigeria. Suggest why nomadic grazing is better suited to seasonal drought than crop farming. Many of the tree plantation crops such as rubber and oil palm need heavy rainfall for most of the year. Why are such crops grown in the south of Nigeria? Why do developing countries find it more difficult economically, to deal with their rainfall patterns?

Fig. 3.37 *Major types of British farming. Why are cereals grown in the east but in the west the main farming is dairying? Why do cereal yields fall towards the north?*

Fig. 3.36 *Farming in Nigeria*

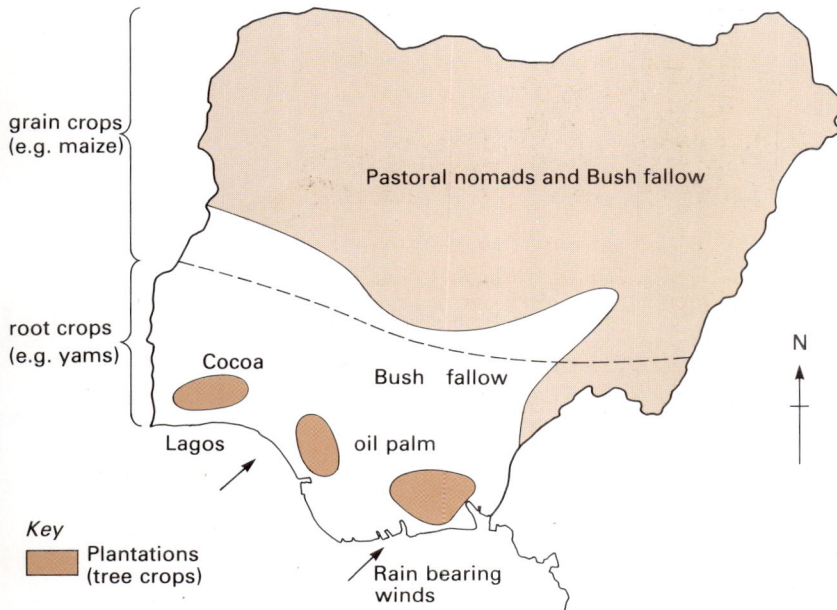

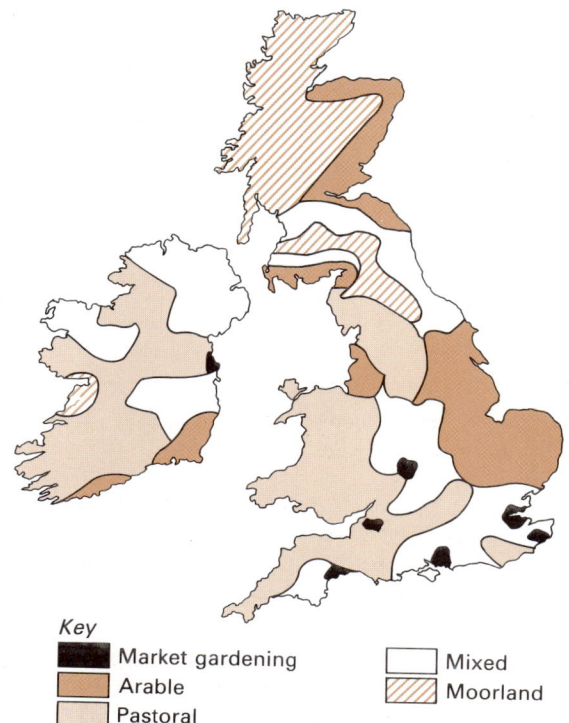

Power

Wind has long been used to turn millstones or to pump water in mills such as that shown in the photograph (fig. 3.39). In California large groups of modern windmills have been built to turn energy into electricity. This source of energy is very cheap once the mills have been built. Why might there be local opposition to the building of such wind farms on nearby high ground?

Another source of energy is solar power. This is unlikely to be used widely in cloudy Britain but is very suitable for many tropical countries. Countries like Britain have very seasonal climates and so the winter's energy demands greatly exceed the summer's. Much has been done to conserve or reduce energy use especially in winter. Find out all you can about energy saving in your home and school.

Transport

A transport terminus may be located to take advantage of climate. Airports are one example. They are located to avoid fog-prone areas and to take advantage of strong prevailing winds for aircraft take-off. Transport routes can be influenced by weather. The M62 route across the Pennines was diverted to avoid the higher ground which was susceptible to high winds and snow drifts. Canal and river transport is influenced by droughts, floods and freezing conditions.

Fig. 3.39 *Windmill*

Fig. 3.38 *Climate graph for Alicante*

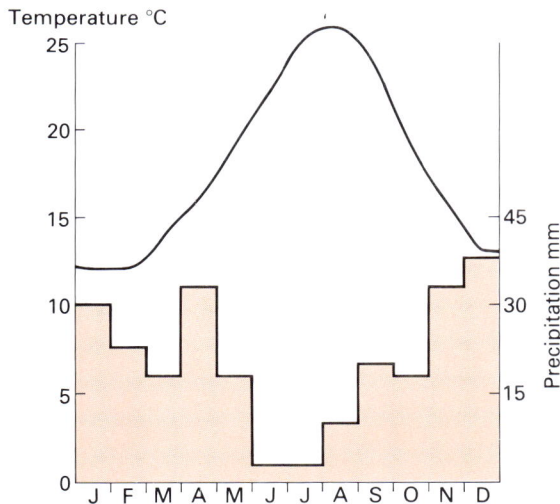

Activities

The weather also influences tourist activities. Look at the climate graph (fig. 3.38) for Alicante in the Mediterranean.
1 When do most visitors from Britain visit the area? Can you explain your answer?
2 Design your own advertisement for Alicante, for display in Britain, stressing the attractions of its climate.
3 Why do you think tropical countries such as Gambia or Nigeria may become major world tourist centres, like Mombassa beach in Kenya has become? Make a collection of travel leaflets on such tropical areas. What do the resorts have in common?

Weather's effects on rocks

Weather can wear down rocks both by erosion, such as wind erosion, and by weathering. Weathering is the destruction of rocks without any moving process being involved.

Mechanical weathering

This is the breaking down of the rock into fragments by changes of pressure within the rock. This type of weathering is common in high latitudes, at high altitudes and in deserts. These changes in pressure may be caused by a number of processes:

1   *Contrasts between hot and cold temperatures*
    In deserts the days are hot with temperatures over 35°C but at night temperatures quickly fall to freezing as there are no clouds to trap in the heat. Daytime heat causes the rock to expand and the cold at night causes sudden contraction. This is repeated until the strain causes the rock to break up. Figure 3.40 shows three types of rock disintegration. Crystals in rocks expand at different rates depending upon their size and colour. Large dark crystals absorb more heat and so expand more until the rock falls apart. Similarly, in jointed rocks each block may expand and contract, and exfoliation occurs when a thin outer layer expands and contracts until it flakes off.
2   *Contrasts between wet and dry*   Many rocks expand when wet but contract and crack as they dry. In what types of weather or climate would this process be common?
3   *Freezing*   If water freezes it expands by 9% in volume and so if water is confined in a

Fig. 3.41 *Frost damage*

crack or joint in a rock it will force the rock apart as it freezes, as shown in fig. 3.41.
4   *Plant roots*   As the roots of plants seek water they can cause great pressure and crack the rock, as shown in figure 3.42. Plant roots are especially active in dry areas as they search for water. Suggest how different plants might differ in the ability of their roots to split rocks.

Fig. 3.42 *Tree rooted in limestone*

Fig. 3.40 *Types of mechanical weathering*

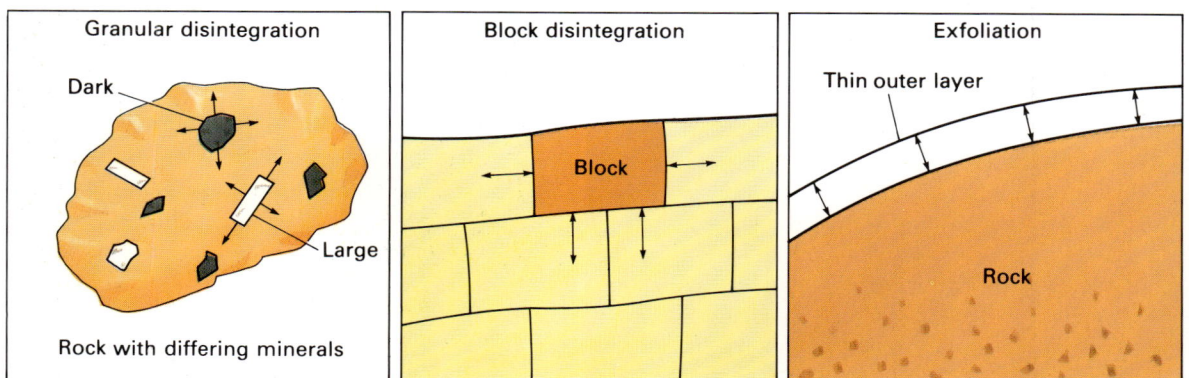

Granular disintegration
Dark
Large
Rock with differing minerals

Block disintegration
Block

Exfoliation
Thin outer layer
Rock

Chemical weathering

A chemical reaction occurs that rots the rock into a sticky residue which is then easily washed away. Some rocks, like rock salt, dissolve in water, but in most cases an acid is needed to rot the rock. Rainwater is a natural weak acid as it contains carbon dioxide which makes carbonic acid, but human activity may increase the acidity of the rain.

Sometimes rocks that contain iron rust in the air while at other times it is the effect of vegetation that produces organic acids which cause the rotting, like that in figure 3.43.

Fig. 3.43 *A Norfolk gravestone – the covering vegetation has been removed!*

Accelerating the weathering

1 *Climate* Look at the graph (fig. 3.44). Explain the differences in the speed and type of weathering in Britain compared to the tropics.

Fig. 3.44 *Impact of climate on weathering*

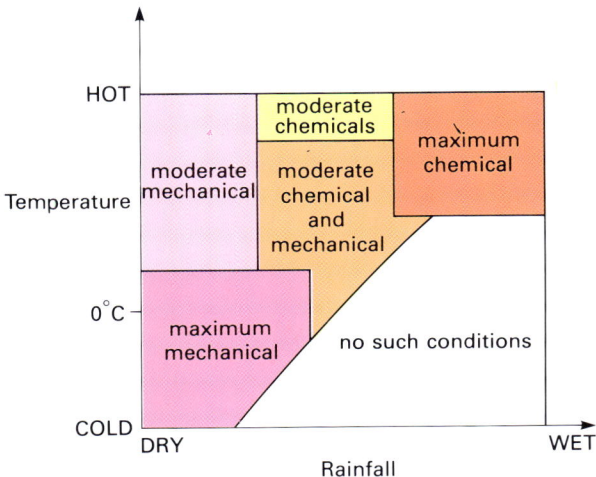

2 *Rock type and structure* Certain rocks contain minerals that dissolve more easily or contain weaknesses such as joints that can be attacked. Why is limestone more easily weathered than slate?

3 *Relief* In areas of steep high relief, such as mountains, the rate of weathering increases due to increased frost action.

4 *Transport* Something is needed to remove the weathered material to expose a fresh surface to attack. What common processes remove debris?

5 *Time* Visit your local graveyard and compare the rate of weathering with the dates on the graves. Do you notice any pattern?

6 *Human activity* This may increase weathering by polluting the air but it can also reduce weathering by protecting exposed surfaces. Look at your own house and school. What is the evidence of weathering? What can be done to reduce it?

Activities

Look at fig. 3.45 which shows the Port Talbot area of South Wales.

1 Draw a sketch section across the map between A and B and label on the steelworks, houses, motorway and damaged hillside.

2 Why do you think the vegetation on the hillside is being killed?

3 Imagine that you live in one of the houses. Describe the problems you would suffer every time it rained. Why might your attitude not be shared by local industrialists?

Fig. 3.45 *Port Talbot area of South Wales*

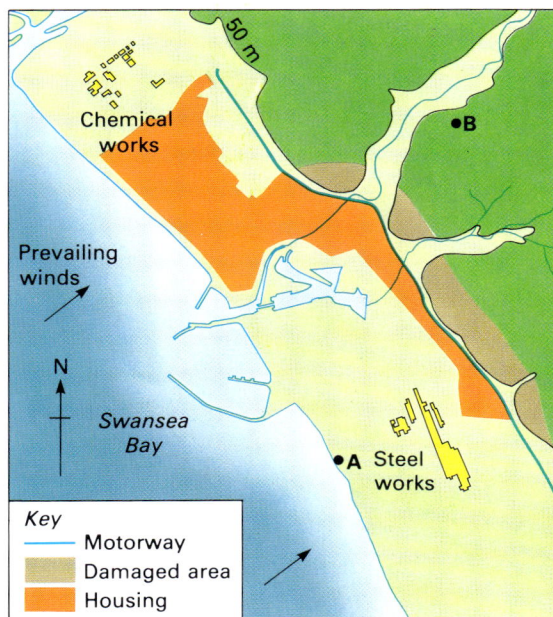

The variations of slopes

Slopes vary in shape and angle. Slopes are systems, and the slope changes when inputs or outputs change, as shown in fig. 3.46. What would happen to the slope if (a) the climate became wetter, or (b) the vegetation was removed?

Rocks and slopes

The type and structure of rock influences slope shape. Hard rocks tend to produce steep slopes and soft rocks tend to produce gentle slopes. Strata or beds of differing hardness may produce ledges or steps, as shown in the photograph (fig. 3.47).

Processes and slopes

Processes also influence slopes. Some processes steepen slopes by undercutting them, like the river in the field sketch (fig. 3.48). Weathering tends to make slopes gentler. The chief processes are the slipping, sliding and flowing movements which together are called mass movement. This movement may be very slow and small scale such as soil creep, or very fast, such as a mudflow. Why is a mudflow so fast?

Fig. 3.46 *The slope system*

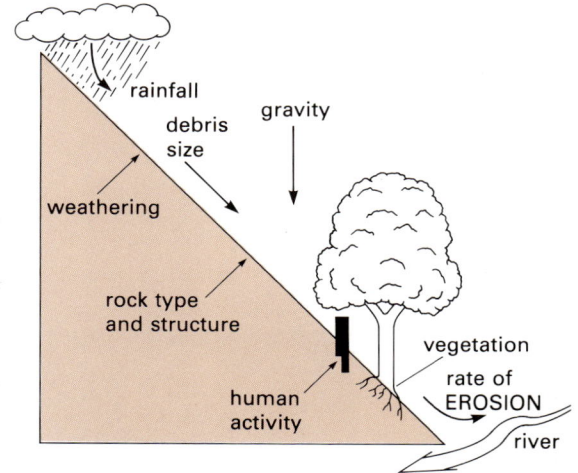

Fig. 3.47 *Yew Coqar Scar in the Pennines. Draw a field sketch of the photograph and label the hard and soft rocks. Why do you think this slope is a hazard?*

Fig. 3.48 *Mass movement at Scaleber near Settle, the Pennines. Explain why mass movement is taking place at this location.*

For mass movement to occur, certain conditions are needed: slopes should be steep, something should undercut the foot of the slope, there should be plenty of water to help lubricate the movement and add weight, and there should be little vegetation to bind the soil.

Sadly these conditions were met on 21 October 1966 at Aberfan in South Wales where an old coal-waste tip flowed down the valley side sweeping over the village school, killing 116 children and 28 adults. Figure 3.49 shows how the disaster occurred.

Fig. 3.49 *Aberfan disaster. What would you have done to reduce the hazard for the school? Who do you think should pay for such a scheme?*

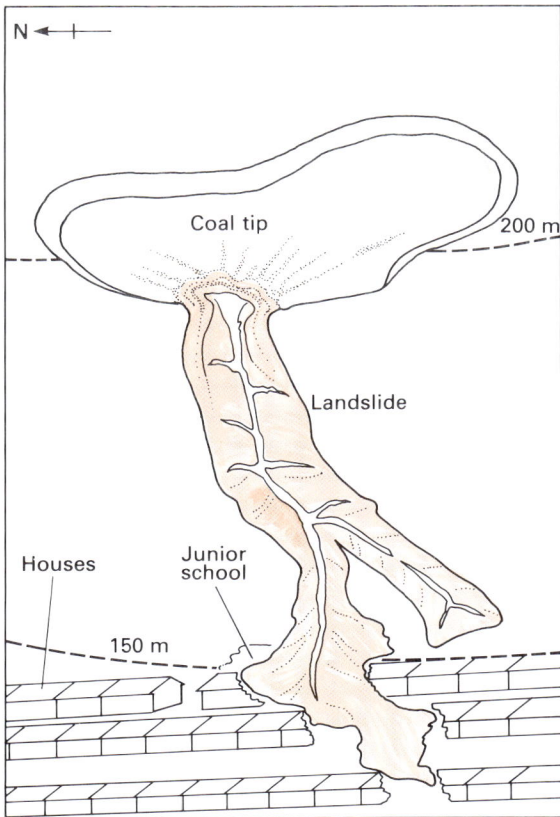

Fig. 3.50 *Hillside in Hong Kong*

Another area with a similar hazard is Hong Kong, as shown in fig. 3.50. In August 1976 heavy rain set off a series of landslides in Hong Kong that killed twenty-two and left thousands homeless.

Slope angle

Slope angle is vital. To exceed the normal angle for an activity is to take a risk. Table 3.51 shows some of the limitations of various slope angles. Clearly, roads and railways sometimes need to have cuttings built to reduce steep slopes, but this can result in landslides if the sides of the cutting are too steep.

Another slope hazard is the avalanche. This is a common hazard on north- and east-facing slopes in mountainous areas. In spring, melting snow causes an increase in weight and lubricates the snow on the steepest slopes. Any sudden shock may set it off. Winter-sports visitors are at particular risk. Try to discover how forests and mortar bombs are used to reduce the risk of avalanches.

Activities

1 Look at fig. 3.50. Why do the people have to build on such steep slopes? Imagine that you are living in this type of housing. Can you describe some of the problems you would encounter?
2 Why are the hill slopes terraced in this way? What would happen if the trees were all cut down?
3 Design a set of policies to prevent people building on these slopes. Write a speech to justify this policy to the people living there.

Fig. 3.51 *Slope limitations. What do you think would happen if you ploughed a slope over 15°?*

Slope angle	
1°	limit for airport runways
2°	limit for motorways, main-line railways
5°	limit for large industrial plants
12°	limit for housing
15°	limit for tractors and ploughing
30°	limit for pastoral farming
45°	limit for forestry

4 RIVER FEATURES AND USES

The water cycle

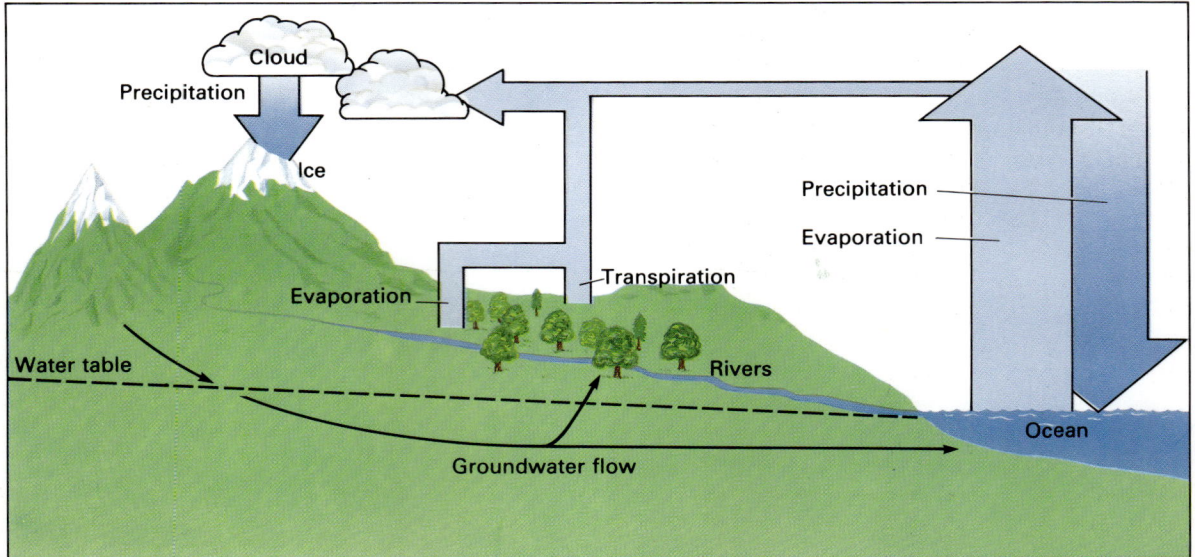

Fig. 4.1 *The water cycle. Why are there no inputs or outputs in this system? How can the cycle be interrupted? What factors might influence the speed of the cycle?*

Fig. 4.2 *Groundwater*

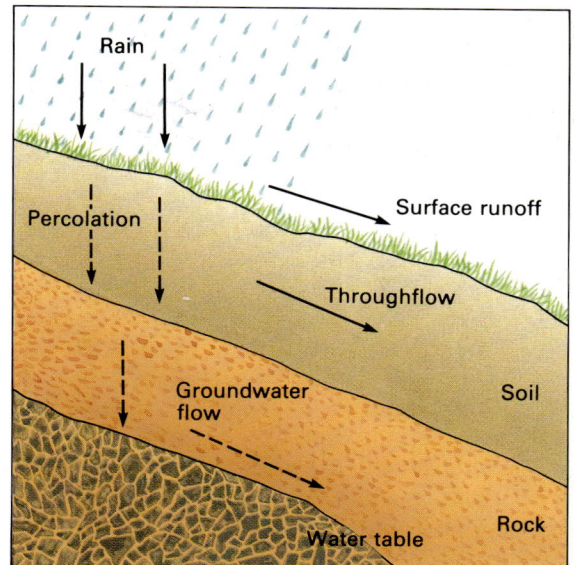

The water cycle is shown in fig. 4.1. This shows a closed system. Oceans are the biggest store of water. The system can be damaged or slowed by human activity, such as the removal of forests and the use of water in industry.

Once the water reaches the ground it may flow away as runoff or seep down into the ground (infiltration). Runoff flows into rivers and lakes from which the water evaporates. The water that has seeped into the ground either flows through the soil (throughflow) or joins the water stored in the soil as groundwater, as shown in fig. 4.2. The rate of movement through the soil depends partly on its porosity and partly on how much water is already in the soil. The water in the soil may reappear as a spring on the surface. People alter this underground water by pumping it for drinking water and by causing pollution. As water evaporates it rises as vapour and is cooled. This cooling causes the water vapour to condense and eventually it forms clouds.

Any further cooling may cause rain and the cycle is complete. Why does the rate of evaporation vary with the climate? How can human activity increase the rate of evaporation?

The graph (fig. 4.3) shows streamflow and precipitation for a small urban stream. Suggest why the precipitation in early January had no real effect on streamflow, but that in late January had a large effect. Streamflow graphs often show a sudden rise as runoff swells the stream and then falls slowly as groundwater and throughflow add their water, which takes longer to reach the stream. How can there be any streamflow when there is no precipitation?

Human activity also has a water cycle, as is shown in fig. 4.5. Waste water is collected in drains and sewers and then processed; 99.9% of the waste is water. Large objects are removed by screening and solids settle out in settlement tanks. Organic waste is removed by filtration and the action of bacteria placed in the filters. The clean water is pumped into storage reservoirs. From here it is treated and pumped to our homes and schools.

Fig. 4.3 *Streamflow and precipitation*

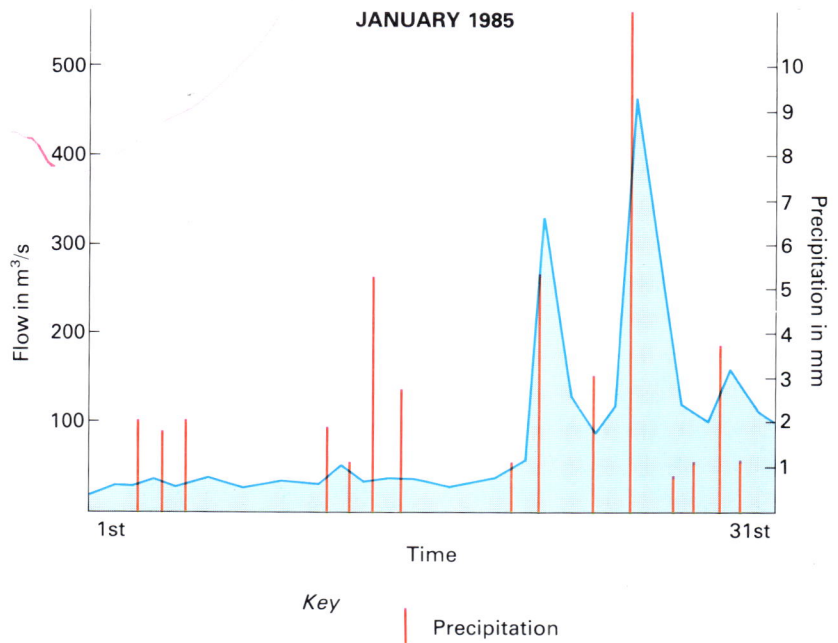

Fig. 4.4 *A water-treatment plant*

Fig. 4.5 *The human water cycle*

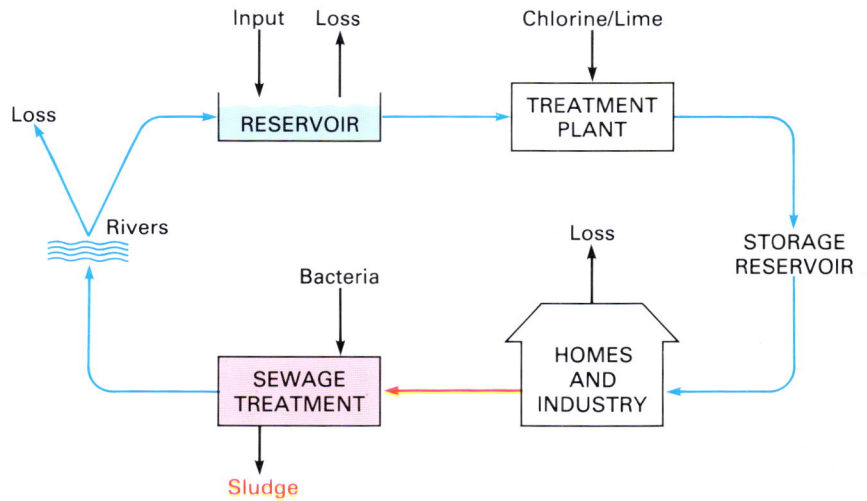

Activities

1 What are the inputs in the human water cycle? Why is this system called an open system?
2 What other uses are there for the water?
3 Imagine that you live near a local water-treatment plant, as shown in the photograph (fig. 4.4). Describe your attitude to the planned extension of the plant.
4 Why should the water be treated before it is pumped into a river or the sea? Find out where your waste water goes.

Rivers' energy

A number of factors affect the river system, as shown in fig. 4.6. Energy is directly related to the speed and volume of the river. The river's first use of this energy is to transport itself by overcoming the friction of its channel sides and bed (cross profile). The river uses its energy to transport itself. If there is any spare energy it will first transport material, and then erode both its banks and bed.

Fig. 4.6 *The river system. Which of the factors influence the volume and which the speed?*

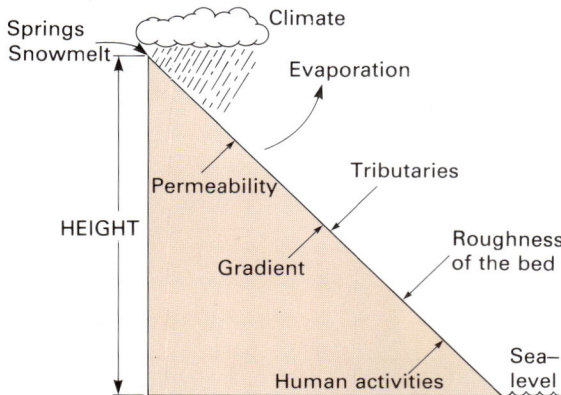

Fig. 4.7 *Cross profiles of river channels*

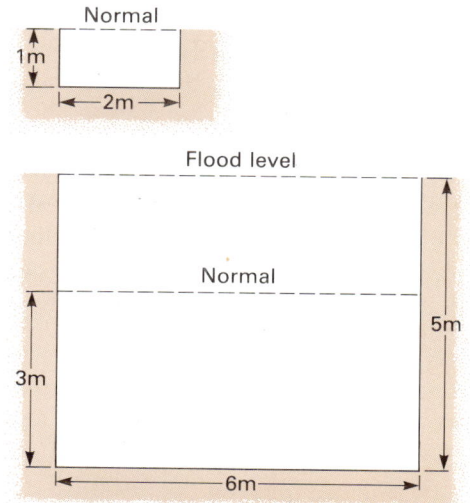

Fig. 4.8 and 4.9 *Rivers with different energy levels*

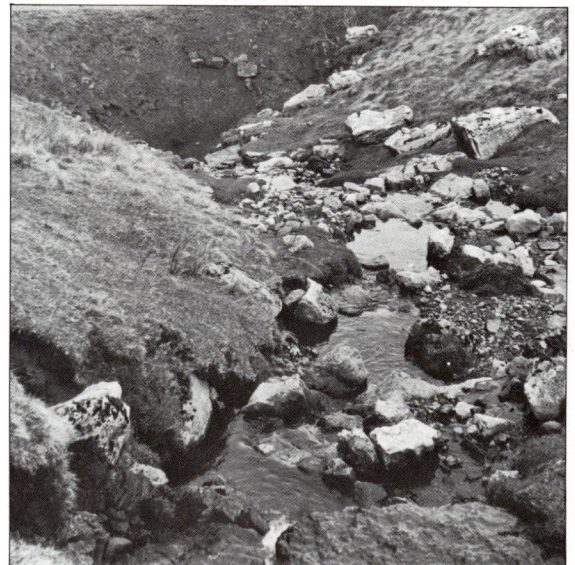

Activities

1 Look at fig. 4.7. Calculate the length of the bed and sides of each of the channels. Compare each of these measurements with the cross-sectional area of the channels. Why is the younger, smaller channel less efficient than the larger one?
2 Can you calculate the difference in the channel between normal and flood levels? What effect do you think this has on the river's speed during a flood?
3 The two photographs (figs. 4.8 and 4.9) show a river near its source and one near its mouth. Make a list of the differences between the two scenes. Explain which river has the most energy.

River erosion

Rivers can erode in a number of ways. Look at fig. 4.10 which shows the main types of erosion. Attrition is the grinding together of pebbles to produce sand-sized particles whilst corrosion swirls pebbles against the bed and banks. Why is the type of rock and its structure important in controlling the type and speed of erosion? With the help of fig. 4.11 suggest when rivers are most erosive. Rivers pick out and erode any weaknesses in the rock to form distinctive features.

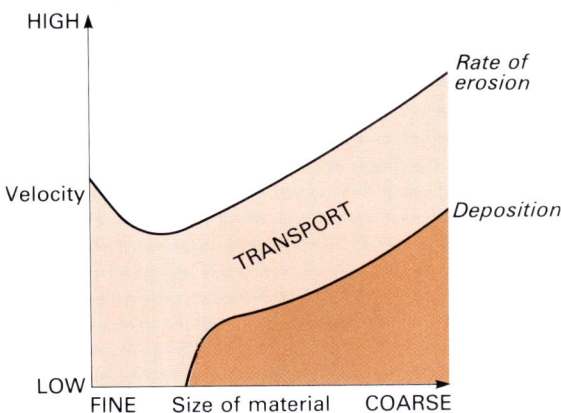

Fig. 4.10 *Main types of river erosion*

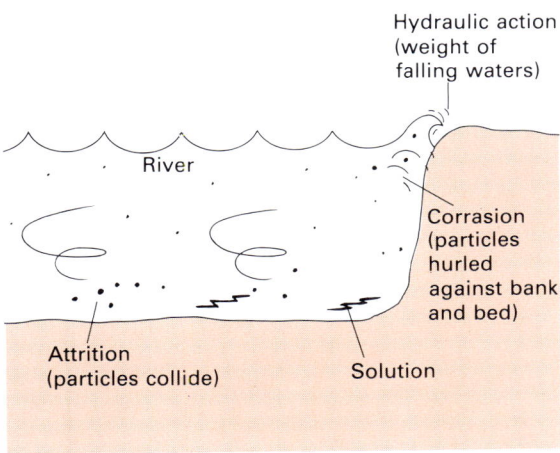

Fig. 4.11 *Velocity and river processes*

Caves

These may occur in highland areas where storm water attacks any weakness in the side of the channel. If the rock is hard enough a cave may form.

Potholes

Whirlpools or eddies in the moving water pick up gravel and swirl it around so eroding any weakness on the river's bed. As the eddies swirl so the gravel is used to drill a circular hole (fig. 4.12). Often the weakness is a joint or bed. They are normally cut during a swirling flood but even at low water the solution process is still eroding them.

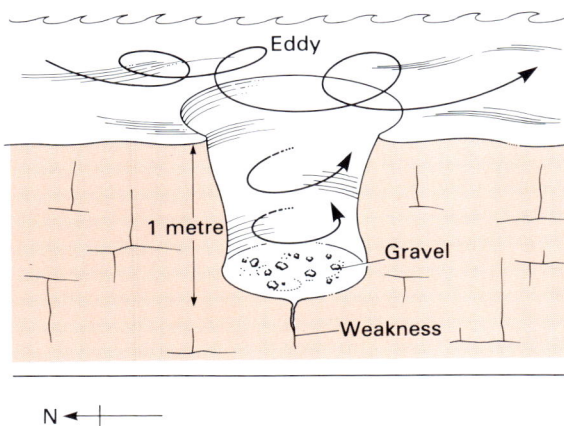

Fig. 4.12 *Pothole formation. Why might potholes be dangerous to bathers?*

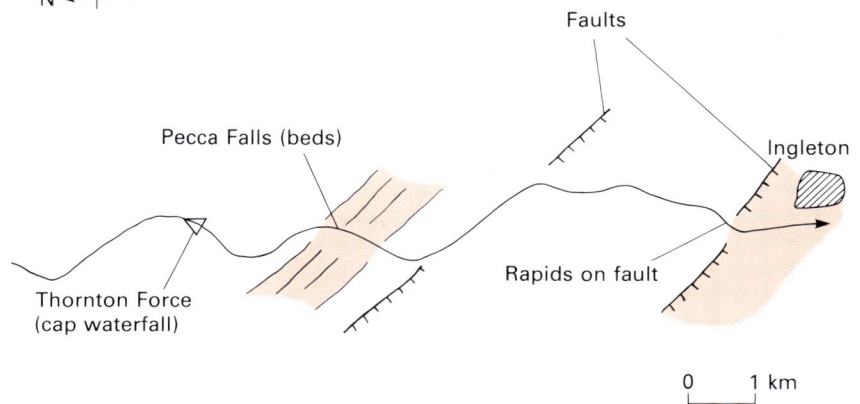

Fig. 4.13 *The Kingsdale Beck in the Pennines*

Waterfalls

The river picks out hard bands or weaknesses in the channel bed but it may lack the power to remove them completely. The river may be forced to fall over them. The exact nature of the falls depends on the rock structure. The falls are most common in highland stretches of rivers where hard rocks are picked out by fast-flowing streams. The map (fig. 4.13) shows a river in the Pennines where numerous waterfalls occur because of the different types

Fig. 4.14 *Thornton Force. What evidence of retreat is shown?*

Fig. 4.15 *Pecca Falls. Why is there a series of falls rather than one waterfall?*

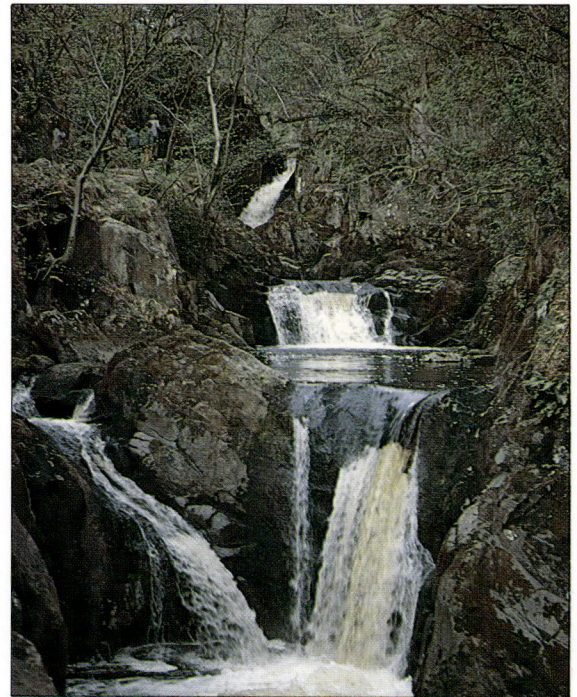

Undercutting is more difficult if the beds of rock slant vertically. These may form vertical-barrier falls such as that formed by the Great Whin Sill – a band of hard volcanic rock – that cuts across the river Tees, as shown in figure 4.16.

Fig. 4.16 *High Force Water, River Tees. Why do these vertical-barrier falls bring both advantages and disadvantages for human activities?*

of rock. Thornton Force (fig. 4.14), is a horizontal-cap waterfall as it has a harder horizontal layer standing out. Water removes the softer or weaker underlying rock so that the cap is left unsupported. It collapses, and the waterfall retreats. As it retreats it leaves a gorge behind.

The Pecca Falls shown in the photograph (fig. 4.15) are a series of falls made by a series of beds of steeply-tilted gritstone.

Valleys

Rivers erode downwards to form valleys but the slope of the valley sides is gradually reduced by weathering. The exact shape of the valley depends not only on the balance between river erosion and weathering but also on the structure of the rock. In the highland stage or near the river's source, downcutting is as rapid as the gradient is steep. So valleys tend to be narrow and deep like that illustrated in the photograph (fig. 4.17). Further down the river the gradient is less and so erosion is less. Weathering begins to make the sides gentler.

Fig. 4.17 *Highland or youthful valley. What evidence is there that the river can flow a lot deeper and faster? Why do you think that valleys like this are left forested?*

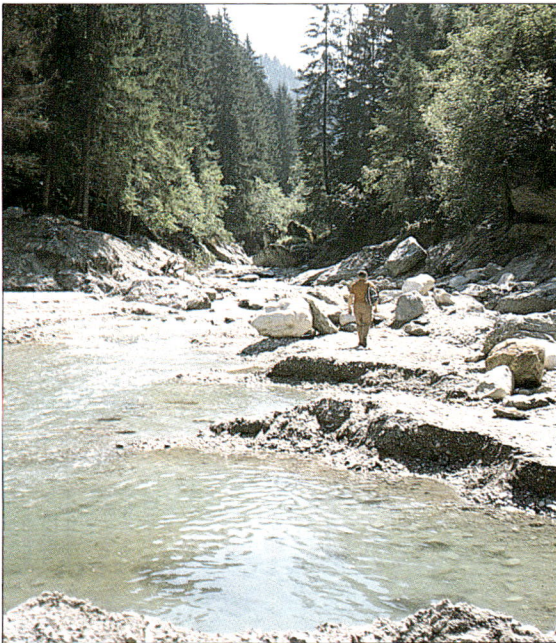

Fig. 4.18 *Valley cross-section, river Wharfe, Bolton Abbey*

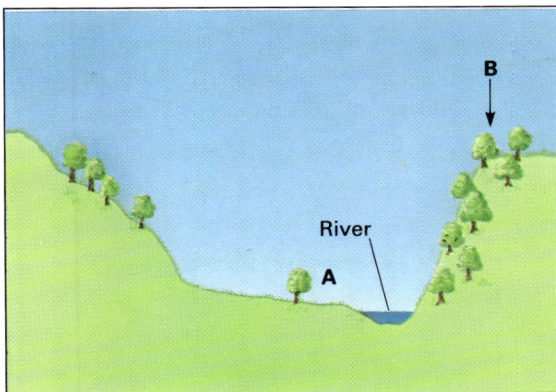

By the time the river has widened and slowed in the flood-plain stage the gradient is so gentle that erosion has nearly stopped. This produces a wide gently sided valley, as shown in fig. 4.19. These plains are often marshy and poorly drained. This may cause major problems for human activity.

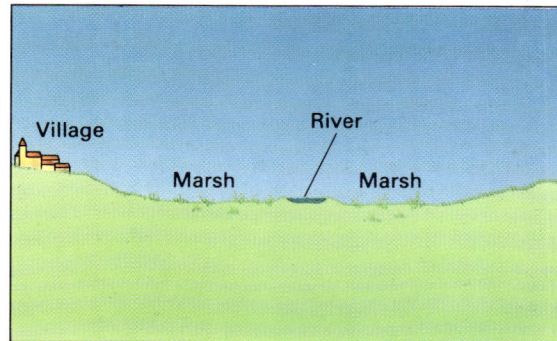

Fig. 4.19 *An old age valley or flood plain. Why are valleys like these called flood plains?*

Sometimes the land rises, the sea-level falls or the climate becomes wetter. This makes the river gain energy again as the gradient is steepened. The river now cuts into the flat flood plain leaving the old level to remain as a terrace. In the case of the river Glaven in Norfolk (fig. 4.20) distinct terraces were left.

Fig. 4.20 *River Glaven at Cley, Norfolk. Why are terraces so useful for human activity?*

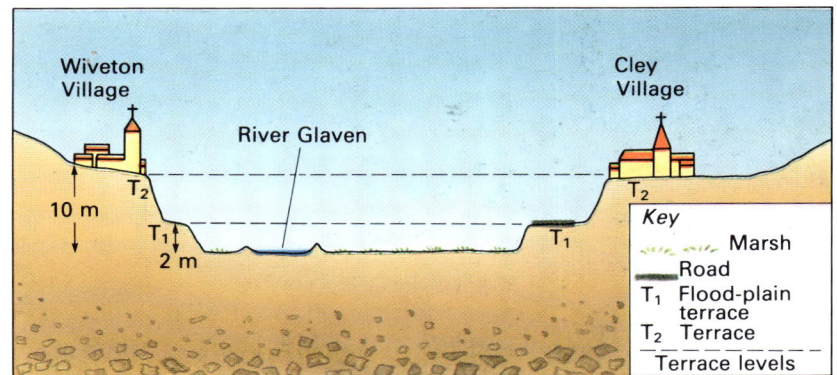

Activities

Look at the valley cross-section (fig. 4.18).
1 Measure the slope angles of the two valley sides. Why is one side steeper than the other?
2 Suggest why you would advise someone not to build a house at either A or B.
3 Why are trees often grown on slope B?

River deposits

As the river loses energy it can no longer carry its load of eroded material. Figure 4.21 shows various causes of energy loss that lead to river deposition. Figure 4.22 shows that the largest and heaviest material is deposited first. Solution load tends to remain dissolved, but what conditions might cause it to be deposited?

Fig. 4.21 *Causes of energy loss. Which do you think is the most common?*

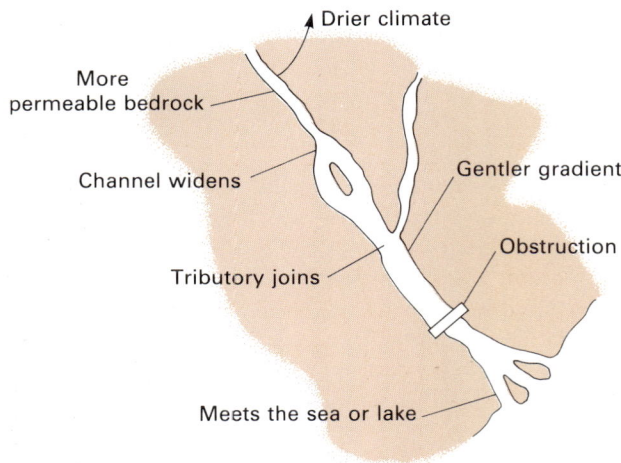

Drier climate
More permeable bedrock
Channel widens
Gentler gradient
Obstruction
Tributory joins
Meets the sea or lake

Fig. 4.22 *Deposition of material*

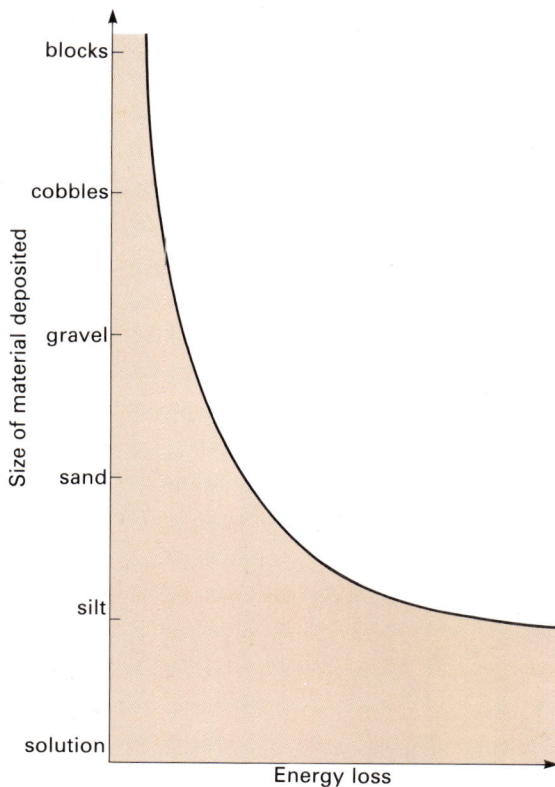

Levées

The Yangtze in China carries over 500 million tonnes of material each year, of which probably 200 million tonnes is deposited along its bed. Deposition may be increased in time of flood. The banks may be built up to form embankments or levées many metres above the flood plain which further increases the risk of flooding of the lower plain on either side, at times of high water volume.

Fig. 4.23 *Local river meander*

Site	A	B	C	D	E
Size of material in mm	25	22	15	6	5

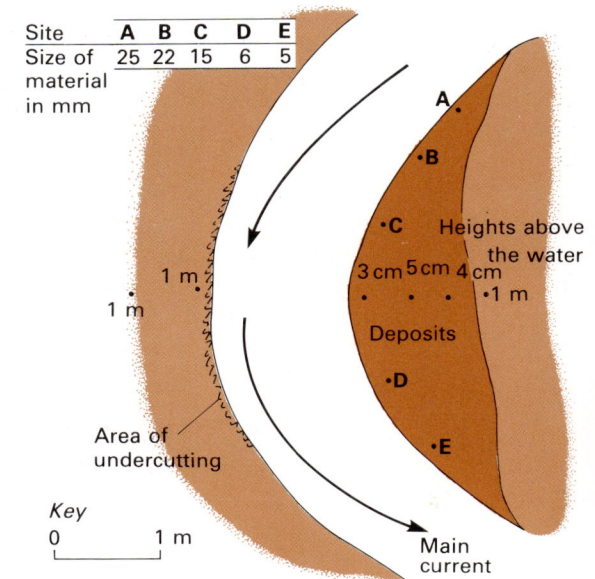

Heights above the water
3 cm 5 cm 4 cm 1 m
Deposits
Area of undercutting
Key 0 — 1 m
Main current

Activities

Figure 4.23 shows a local river bend or meander.
1 Draw a section across the river and label the areas of deposition and erosion.
2 Draw a graph to show the average sizes of material deposited from A to E. Why does the size vary?
3 What effect will this erosion and deposition have on the course of the river? Why might this be important for natural or local boundaries?

Backswamp

Once the floodwater has left the higher river channel it cannot return uphill so spreads out across the low-lying areas. It gradually evaporates leaving a marshy area known as a backswamp, as shown in fig. 4.24. In some countries this marshy area is of great economic benefit, being used for intensive farming, often of rice.

Braid

Sometimes the whole river has to slow down, often when the gradient lessens or a tributary joins. Most debris is carried in the centre, where the water is fastest, so when the river slows it deposits most material in the centre of its channel. This may eventually build up into a small island or braid. Some braids can be very big. The examples shown in the map (fig. 4.25) have been extensively affected by human activity.

Deltas

The most spectacular examples of braiding occur when a river meets the sea and a delta forms. Ideal conditions for delta formation occur in the Mediterranean, as shown in the map (fig. 4.26). Here the rivers are slow, full of silt, and the sea is relatively calm, with few tides or currents. As the river deposits, it can speed up because it has reduced its load and reduced its channel width. This enables the river to flow further out into the sea. This may be repeated many times until the delta extends far out into the sea. The Yangtze delta is advancing at 1 km every forty years. Not all rivers produce deltas.

Activities

1 Make a list of European rivers without deltas. Why do you think that the Thames has no delta?
2 Make a list of the advantages and disadvantages that the growth of a delta might bring.
3 Present the attitudes of a naturalist and a farmer to the proposed reclamation of a delta areas.

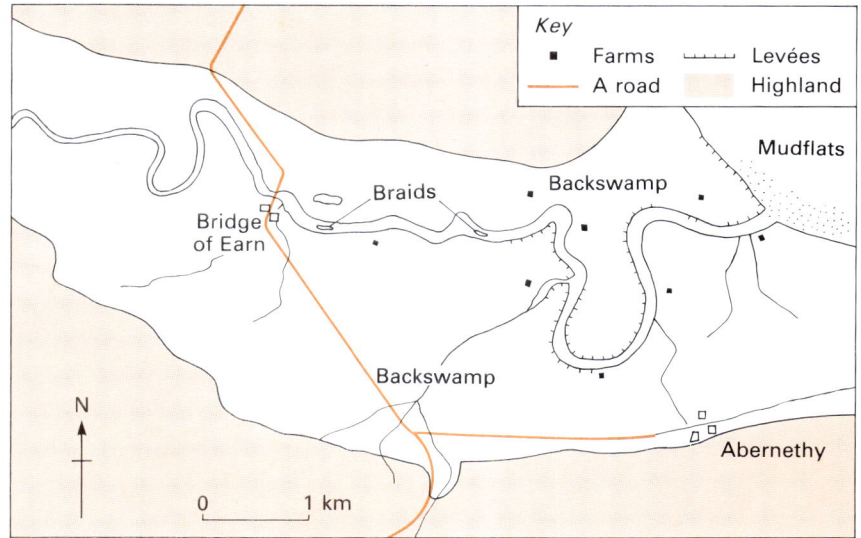

Fig. 4.24 *The river Earn, in Scotland – a river in old age. How has the marshy area affected the location of roads and settlements?*

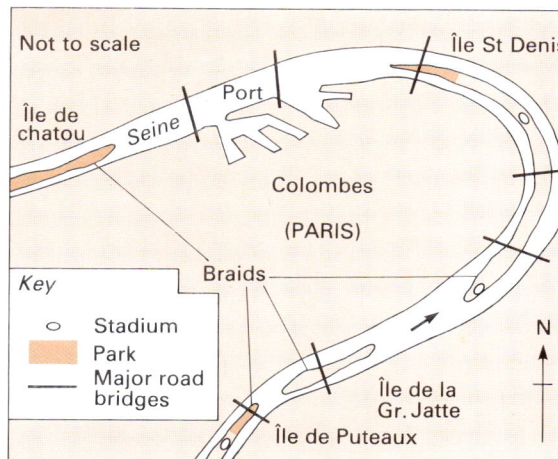

Fig. 4.25 *Braids on the river Seine in Paris. Why might living on a braid like one of these be risky?*

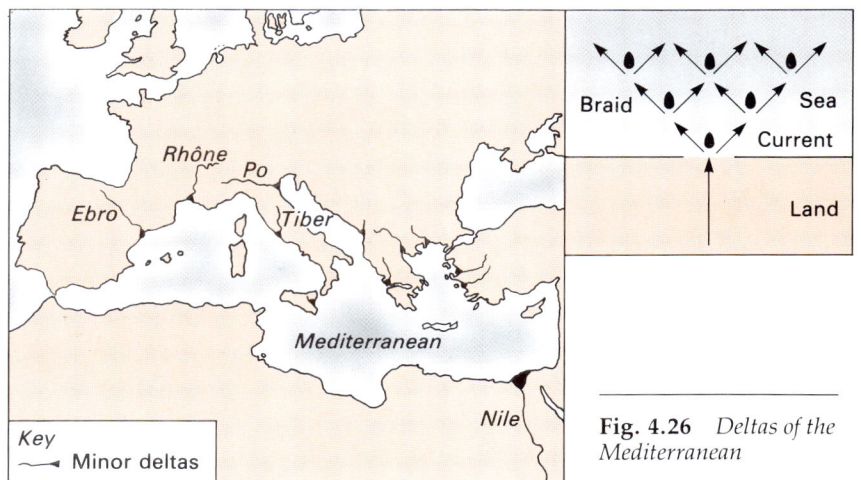

Fig. 4.26 *Deltas of the Mediterranean*

River hazards

Fig. 4.27 *The Lyn rivers, Exmoor. Why was the flood so powerful?*

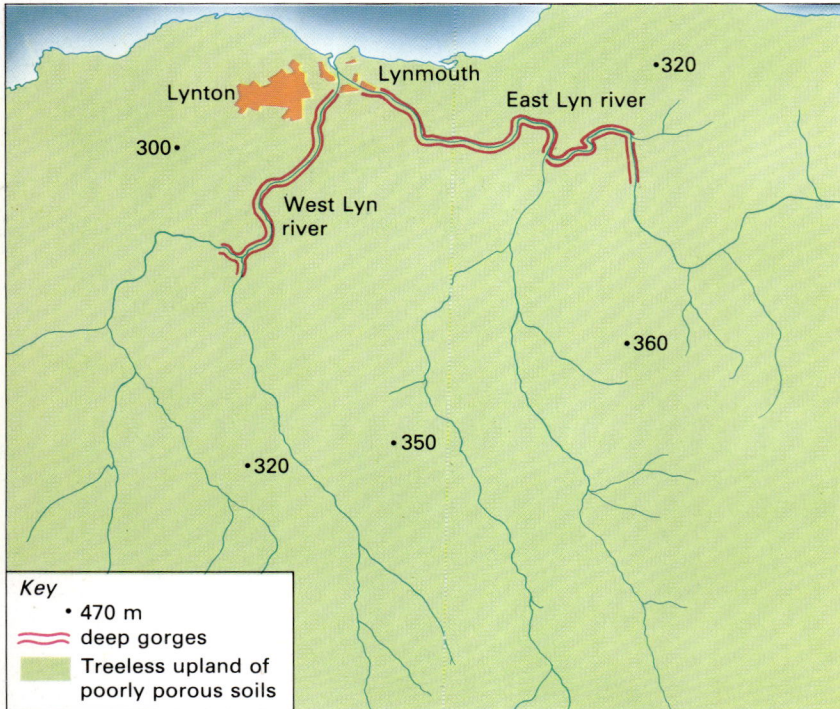

Key
- 470 m
- ∿∿ deep gorges
- Treeless upland of poorly porous soils

Fig. 4.28 *The Yangtze, China*

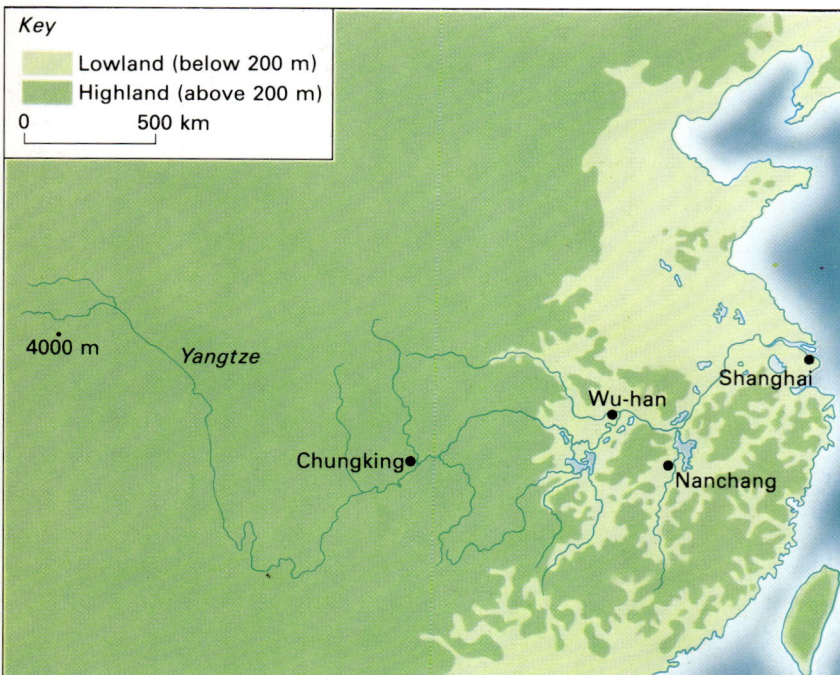

Key
- Lowland (below 200 m)
- Highland (above 200 m)
- 0 ___ 500 km

Floods

Rivers can flood in any of their stages following heavy rain or sudden melting of snow. In August 1952, 228 mm of rain fell in twelve hours on Exmoor and this led to the tiny Lyn rivers becoming so enlarged in their deep, restricted valleys that when the floodwater reached the village of Lynmouth it destroyed nearly 100 houses and drowned thirty-four people. The force of the water was sufficient to move boulders weighing over 4 tonnes. Look at the map of the area (fig. 4.27), and work out why the flood was so powerful.

The most disastrous floods have been in the lower reaches of rivers because of the massive volumes of water and excessively meandering or winding courses. The map (fig. 4.28) shows the Yangtze in China. The river floods from March to November every year following the melting of snow and monsoon rains in the highlands. The river is 5525 km long with eight major tributaries. Also in the flood-plain area it has built up levées 2–3 m above the level of the land. The flood plain contains nearly 30% of the population of China and the area grows 45% of China's rice. Suggest why this area is prone to damaging floods. The flooding is so regular that the local population have adapted to it and use it to irrigate crops. Since 1954, 20 000 kms of dykes have been built to control the floods. Why might these increase the risk of flooding in some areas, and how do you think the numerous lakes could help reduce flood risk?

Human reaction to flooding is rather limited. People have short memories or do not realise the risk. Many people live in risky areas because they gain benefits from a riverside location. What benefits could such an area offer?

Flood prevention

Floods can be reduced by reinforcing embankments, as shown in the photograph (fig. 4.29). Concrete blocks linked by tar are used to reduce the erosion of the earth embankments. A ditch on the land side of the wall collects any seepage through the embankment.

Fig. 4.29 *East coast river defences. How can human activity damage these defences?*

Fig. 4.30 *The Prittlebrook, Southend*

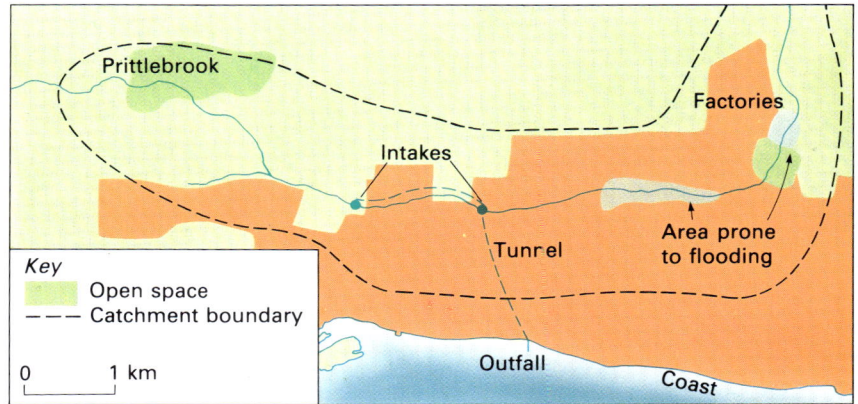

Key
Open space
Catchment boundary
0   1 km

In some cases land is set aside to be deliberately flooded to reduce the pressure on other areas. The Somerset Levels and areas in the Wash are still used for this purpose. Sometimes diversions are built to take away the flood water. Look at the map (fig. 4.30). In September 1968 this small 'urban' stream overflowed, following heavy rain, and flooded 470 houses to a depth of 1 m. It damaged factories and cut all the bridges across the stream.

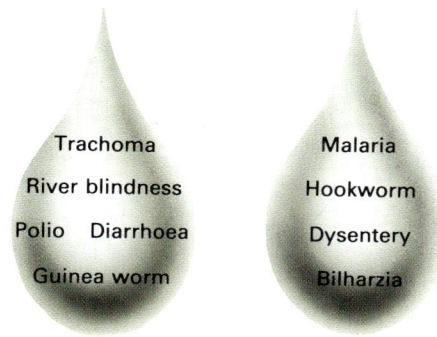

Trachoma
River blindness
Polio   Diarrhoea
Guinea worm

Malaria
Hookworm
Dysentery
Bilharzia

Fig. 4.31 *Major waterborn diseases*

Activities

1 Imagine that your house is flooded. Describe the damage done.
2 What factors increase the risk in urban areas?
3 Look again at fig. 4.30. A 30 m diameter tunnel was driven underground to lead any flood water off to the sea. The cost of this diversion was nearly £500 000. Why do you think such an expensive scheme was justified for such a minor river?

Other river hazards

Rivers can also be hazards in tropical countries because they may increase disease. Figure 4.31 lists some of the major waterborne diseases. Many of these diseases infect people who bathe in or drink from the rivers, and some are carried by insects that live in wet areas. Suggest why tropical countries can do little to control this hazard. Figure 4.32 shows the population pattern and the major rivers in West Africa. Rivers can also be a hazard for transport either crossing or travelling along the river. Waterfalls, sandbanks, shallows and water vegetation all hamper navigation in West Africa.

Fig. 4.32 *Population along the river Niger, West Africa. Why do you think people avoid the river Niger in Nigeria, but were attracted to the same river in Mali and Niger?*

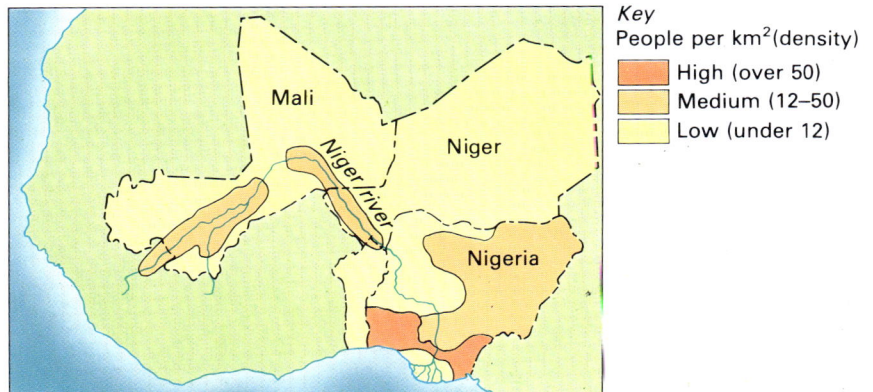

Key
People per km²(density)
High (over 50)
Medium (12–50)
Low (under 12)

Human influence on rivers

The course

Human activity has long altered the courses of rivers. In the 1640s Vermuyden (a Dutchman) cut the Bedford river for 34 km from Earith to Denver, as shown on the map (fig. 4.33) of the English Fens. The New Bedford river was cut in 1650 and since then further cuts have been made. These artificial drainage rivers have had a major effect on the land, producing a flat landscape divided by straight ditches.

On a more local scale, many small streams have their courses 'fixed' by concrete, like that in the photograph (fig. 4.34), or diverted into storm drains. This fixing is needed to reduce erosion of the banks and damage to the surrounding area.

Fig. 4.35 *The Colorado dams*

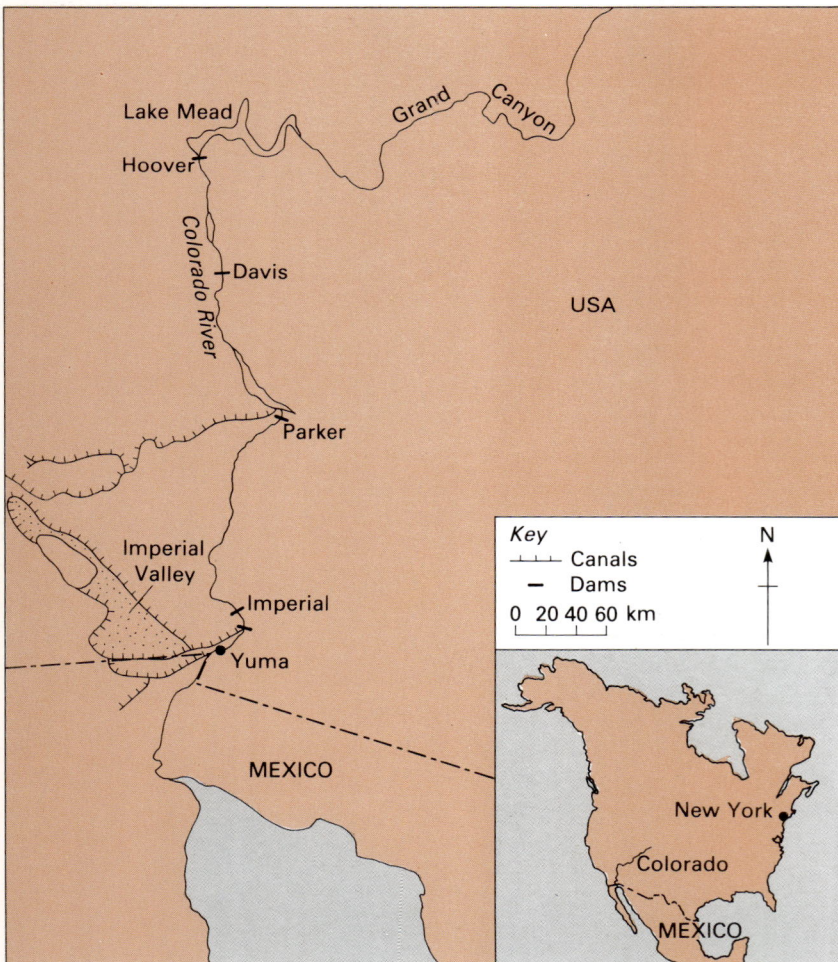

Fig. 4.33 *Simplified drainage map of the fens. How did straightening the rivers help riverflow? These cuts were expensive to dig. Who do you think got the benefits of them?*

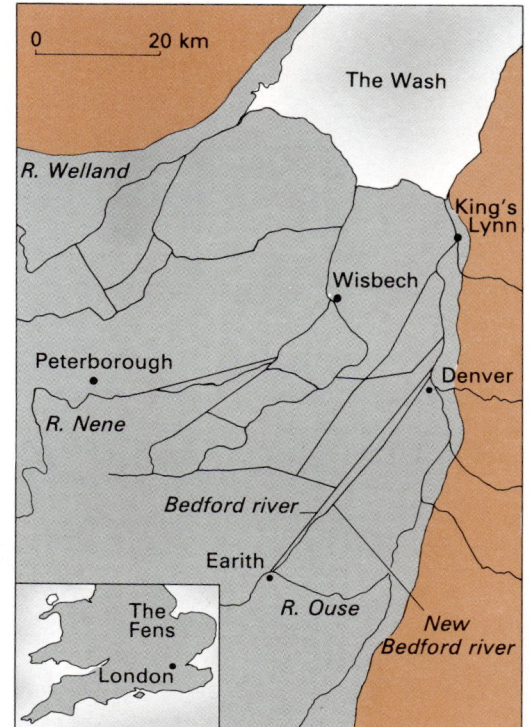

Fig. 4.34 *Local stream controls. What problems might this control of the river produce?*

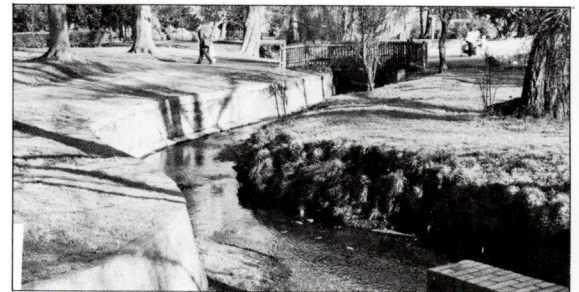

The volume

The building of roads and houses covers the soil with impervious concrete and tarmac. This increases the rate of riverflow as runoff increases because so little water can sink into the soil. The removal of woodland would also increase the rate of runoff. Riverflow can be reduced by dam building and water extraction. The map (fig. 4.35) shows the river Colorado in

North America. Many dams were built on the river to tap irrigation water for this dry and thirsty area as well as to produce water to transfer to other areas.

What would your attitude be if you were a Mexican farmer needing irrigation water? In 1944 a treaty allocated 19 billion m^3 of water to the USA each year, and 1.9 billion m^3 to Mexico, but the riverflow has now fallen to less than 18 billion m^3! This reduction in flow has led to an increased salt content in the water reaching Mexico, and now no water from the Colorado reaches the sea.

The load

Dam construction blocks the transport of the load. The Aswan Dam traps 92% of the silt coming down the Nile. The Dam may eventually become silted up. Human activity can encourage this deposition in order to create new land for farming, as in the case of the Yangtze, or for industrial development. Much of the port and industry in Rotterdam is built on material reclaimed from the river Rhine.

Human activity can increase the river's load by using the river to transport debris. Mines have long used water and rivers to remove waste. Many factories dump waste water or liquids into rivers. These may provide organic matter which serves as food for oxygen-consuming bacteria. These may remove the oxygen from the water reducing the animal life of the river, as shown in fig. 4.36. Some waste solids destroy river-bed life whilst some heavy metals, like copper, are poisonous to life. If fertilisers drain into the water they may stimulate the growth of surface algae which block out the light, and the growth of weed which may choke the river.

Fig. 4.36 *Reduction of life in rivers*

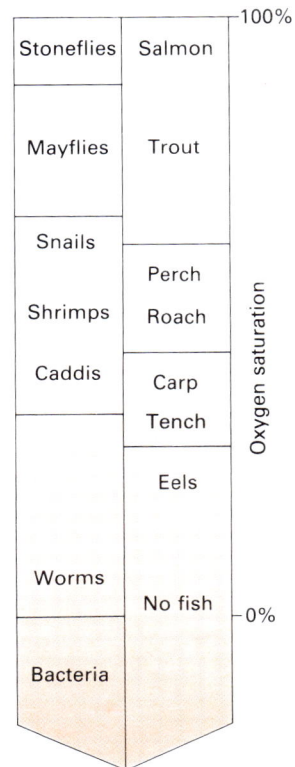

Activities

The map (fig. 4.37) shows Lake Erie in North America. It serves as a waste dump for 13 million people. By 1970 the evidence for the changed nature of the water included dead fish, a stinking scum of algae and a falling local fish catch.
1 How do you think industry and the nature of the local rivers and the nature of the lake, helped to cause the problem?
2 Suggest the different attitudes of an industrialist and a lakeside tourist manager to solving this problem.
3 Why do lakes become more easily polluted than river systems? Why are seas like the Mediterranean also under threat?

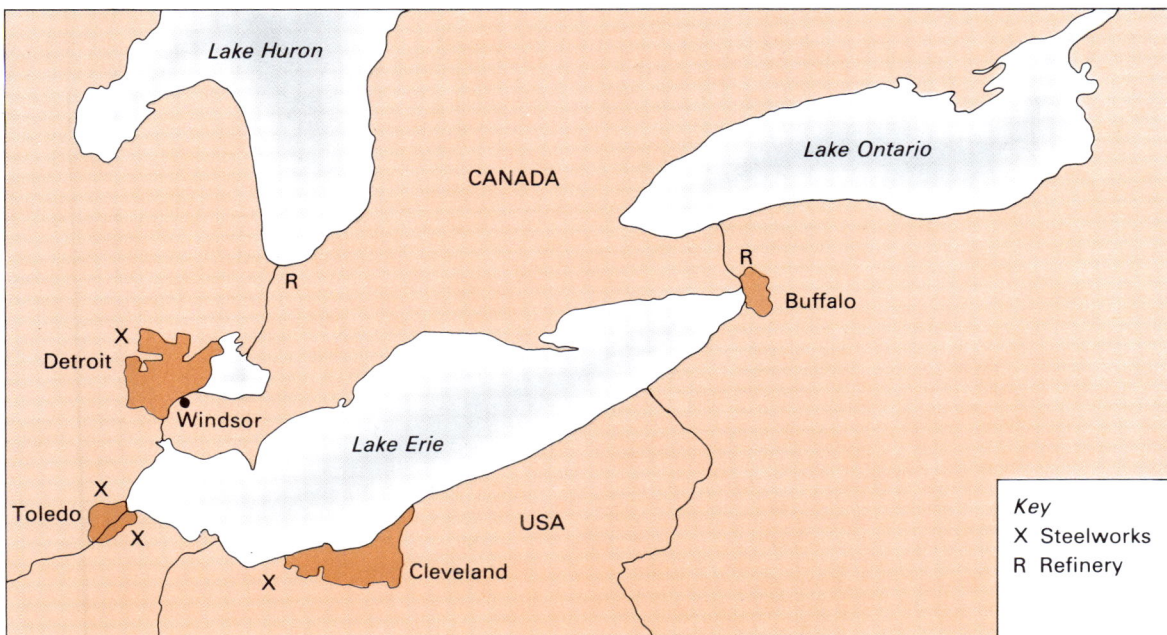

Fig. 4.37 *Lake Erie in North America*

River uses

Raw materials

1 *Minerals*   As river erosion washes out minerals from rocks in its bed these minerals will collect when the river deposits. These stream-bed minerals provide placer deposits and these have long been used for mineral extraction. Clear Creek in Kansas yielded $100 million worth of gold between 1860 and 1920. Today placer deposits are still important: 70% of the world's tin production comes from them. Why do you think they are so easy to mine?

2 *Sand and gravel*   Rivers sort out eroded material and deposit it in graded banks. Look at the photograph of gravel workings (fig. 4.38). Much of the gravel is used in the building industry. The large holes left by gravel digging often become flooded and are used as recreational areas. One of the most spectacular examples of this is Thorpe Park in Surrey.

3 *Rushes and willows*   These have long been harvested. Some of the rushes are used in thatching. Willow is used for basket-making, fencing and cricket bats.

Fig. 4.38 *Gravel workings. Why do you think many people object to these being opened up near to where they live?*

Power

The energy rivers have can be used by humans. Large volumes of water or waterfalls can be harnessed to supply power. In the past, water mills, like that in the photograph (fig. 4.39), were used to extract the power. They worked flour mills, saw mills and drove early textile machinery.

Today river energy is converted into electricity. River flow is used to turn a turbine. This type of power is called hydroelectricity.

Fig. 4.39 *Watermill at Calborne, Isle of Wight*

Sites for these power schemes are either in narrow gorges to reduce the width of the dam needed, as in the case of the Hoover Dam on the Colorado, or where there is a large volume of water, as in the case of the power stations on the river Rhine.

Frequently these schemes are part of a multi-purpose river scheme to help reduce the

Activities

Refer to fig. 4.40
1 Make a list of any other uses for the lake water and the dam. Why do you think such schemes are called multi-purpose?
2 What are the disadvantages of creating such a lake in a tropical country? What are the advantages of hydroelectric power to a developing country like Nigeria?
3 Imagine you are president of a poor country. Write a speech to justify the cost of such a scheme when many of your people are starving.

cost of power production. The Kainji scheme in Nigeria, shown in fig. 4.40, was begun in 1964 and officially opened in 1969. The lake water is used to drive twelve turbines and to provide irrigation water for the surrounding area.

Fish

Many inland countries rely heavily on river fish as a source of protein. The fish are caught using nets, weirs (kinds of dam across rivers), and in the Amazon the natives use spears or even poison from plants to stun the fish. In Britain, salmon and trout are the chief commercial and sport river fish. Many streams have been re-stocked to ensure that they continue to have fish.

Transport

Rivers have been used for transport for a long time. Water reduces the effective weight of any load and so is ideal for boats with heavy and bulky cargoes. Explain why river transport is so suitable for a poor or developing country. Rivers can be improved for transport. In the case of the Rhine, in its rift-valley stage, as shown in fig. 4.41, a series of loop canals were dug and locks built. These loops helped navigation by avoiding shallow areas of the river and also by speeding up the flow, they

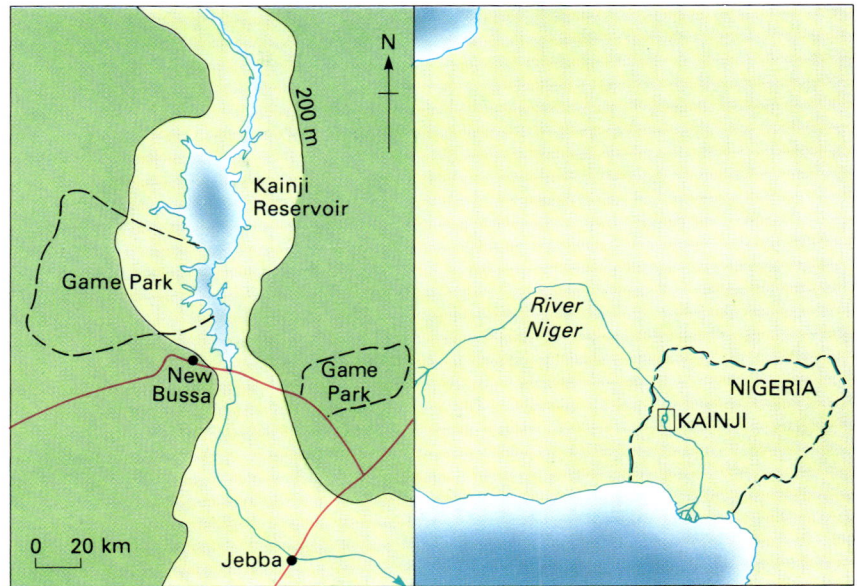

Fig. 4.40 *The Niger river dam at Kainji, Nigeria*

helped to produce power. Locks are used to pass around the dams.

The Rhine is the major routeway of Europe and its importance has been increased by a system of canals, as shown in fig. 4.42. The river is navigable for 800 km and has been an international waterway since the Treaty of Vienna in 1815. Cargoes carried include bulk loads of coal, gravel, iron ore and some manufactured goods.

Fig. 4.41 *A Rhine loop canal. Why are locks sometimes a problem on rivers?*

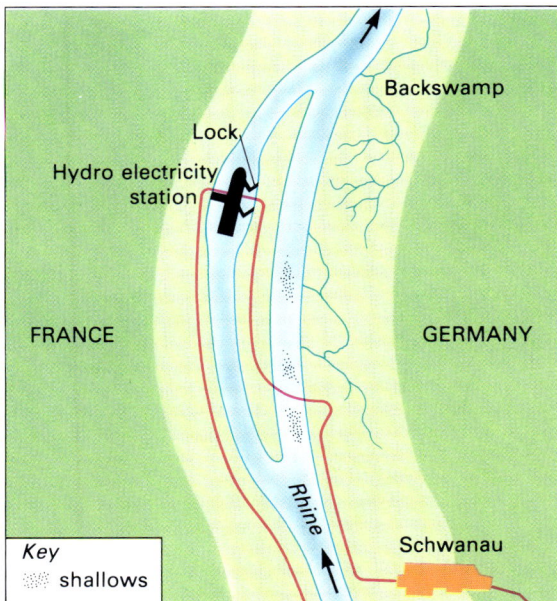

Fig. 4.42 *The Rhine system. Why was a treaty needed before the river could be used?*

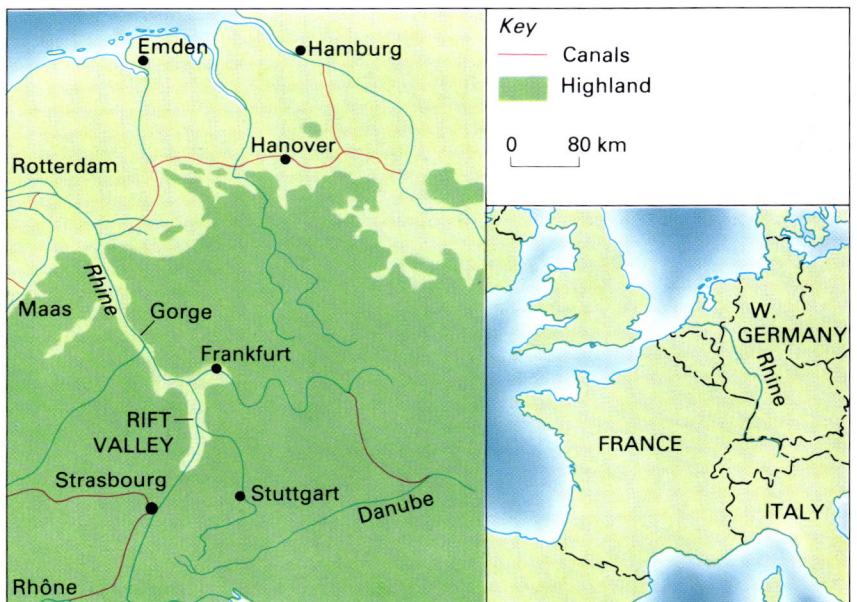

Water supply

The exact balance between the various sources of water varies from area to area.

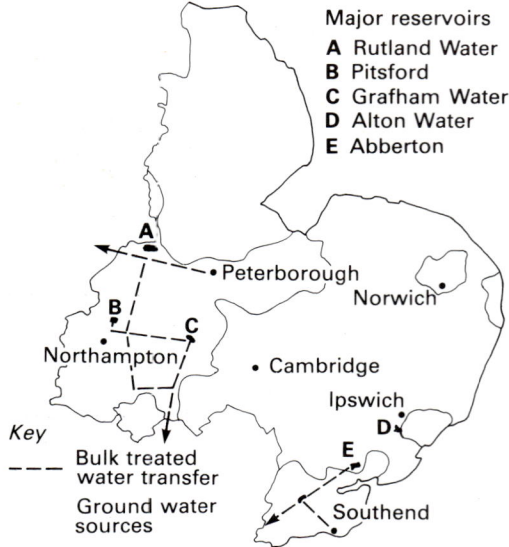

Major reservoirs
A Rutland Water
B Pitsford
C Grafham Water
D Alton Water
E Abberton

Key
— — — Bulk treated water transfer
Ground water sources

Underground sources

Much of the Anglian Water Authority's area takes water from porous underlying rocks, as shown in fig. 4.43. The chief porous rock is chalk. Some of the water comes directly from rainfall but much is drawn in underground from the Wash system of rivers to the west.

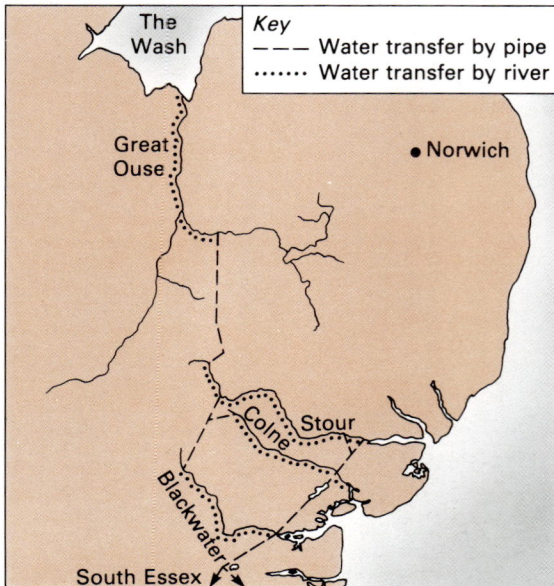

Key
— — — Water transfer by pipe
.... Water transfer by river

Rivers and lakes

Water is taken directly from rivers. In the case of Anglian Water rivers are used to transfer water from areas of plenty to areas of shortage. Figure 4.44 shows the Ely–Ouse–Essex system which was built in the 1970s to transfer water from the Ouse to southern Essex. This area has a large and growing population and many industrial demands, such as oil refineries, but it lacked sufficient local-water supplies. The Anglian Authority has created several artificial lakes to meet local needs. Look at fig. 4.43 again and suggest why the various reservoirs were created. Often the creation of such lakes causes problems by flooding valuable farmland and even villages.

The map (fig. 4.45) shows Rutland Water. Make a list of the activities around the lake. These can conflict with the need to supply clean pure water and they can even conflict with each other. Many of the large natural lakes of Wales and the Lake District are used as reservoirs for areas like the Midlands. What problems can such water transfers bring to both the exporting and receiving area?

Fig. 4.45 *Rutland Water*

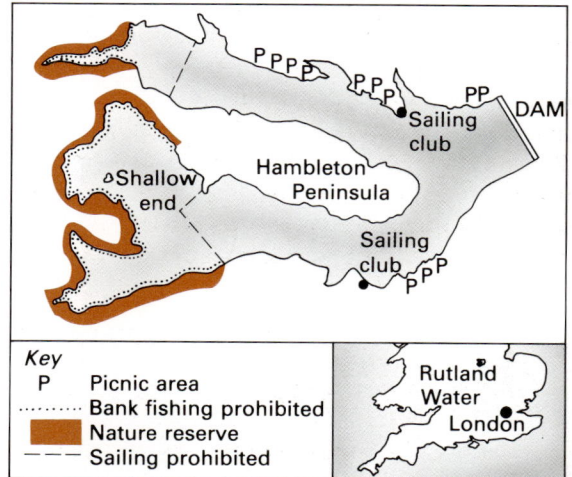

Key
P Picnic area
.... Bank fishing prohibited
■ Nature reserve
— — — Sailing prohibited

Springs

These occur where porous rocks reach the surface, as shown in fig. 4.46. Unfortunately these are an unreliable source of water as they are so influenced by the weather.

Fig. 4.46 *Underground sources of water*

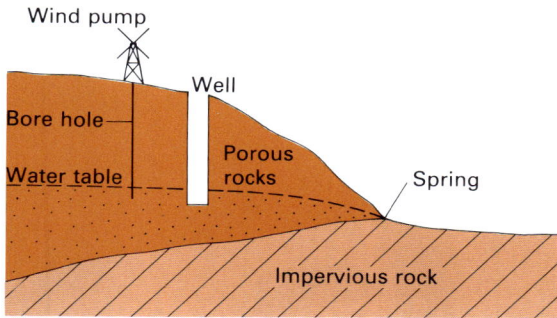

Fig. 4.46 *Underground sources of water*

Various water-saving schemes have been tried. Make a list of how this could be done in your home or school.

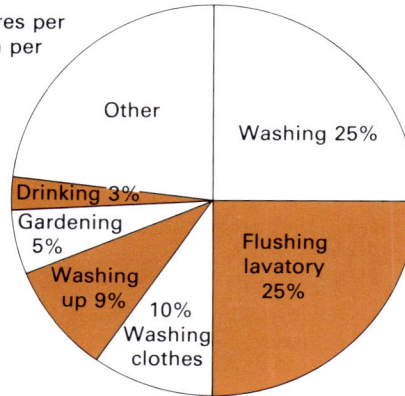

Fig. 4.47 *Domestic uses of water*

Uses

Industry uses water for cleaning, cooling and to put into products. It takes 40 000 litres of water to make a car but 35 000 litres of this are recycled. Domestic uses are shown in fig. 4.47. The average person uses 200 litres each day but as income rises, so water consumption rises. Suggest why this happens. What are the implications for poor but developing countries?

Other water supplies

Water supply needs to be increased. There are plans to create a dam or barrage across estuary areas like the Wash in Britain to create a large reservoir. Such a scheme could also be used to reclaim land and act as a recreational area. Kuwait, on the shores of the Persian Gulf, has no natural supply of freshwater and a rainfall of only 100 mm/year. In 1950, the first desalinisation plant was built to produce 3000 m^3/day. Now plants produce over 90 000 m^3. There are many methods of removing the salt, including evaporating the water and then condensing it. This may also deposit many valuable minerals.

Fig. 4.48 *Anglian Region water supply*

	Anglian region (average year)	Rest of England and Wales (average year)
Rainfall	595 mm	940 mm
Actual evaporation	448 mm	453 mm
Effective rainfall	147 mm	487 mm

Fig. 4.49 *Anglian Region water uses*

	National average	Anglian region
Public water supply	31.7%	53%
Central Electricity Generating Board	43.7%	25%
Other industry	23.3%	17%
Spray irrigation, agriculture and miscellaneous	1.3%	5%
Total	100%	100%

Activities

1 Look at the table (4.48) showing rainfall patterns. Draw pie charts to compare the Anglian Region with the rest of England and Wales in terms of effective rainfall and evaporation. Why is the rainfall low and evaporation high in East Anglia?
2 Why is rainfall a major source of water supply in areas like Wales?
3 Use pie charts to compare the Anglian and National uses of water from table 4.49. Why does the Anglian area use a much greater percentage in agriculture but less in industry and power generation?

Rivers and recreation

Fishing

Rivers are an attraction for many anglers, and angling is the largest participation sport in Britain. The most spectacular area for this activity is Ireland with over 14 000 km of rivers. The game fishing for trout and salmon is some of the best in Europe. Many of the rivers have been stocked by the Inland Fisheries Trust. Look at the advertisement (fig. 4.50) for fishing holidays.

Fig. 4.51 *White water canoeing. Why do you think this activity has little impact on the river or the economy of the area?*

Boating

The nature of the river will largely determine the type of boating. The upland torrents of areas such as Scotland make exciting water for white water canoeing, as shown in the photograph (fig. 4.51). In contrast, mature rivers attract cruising. In summer, the Thames between Windsor and Oxford has more boat traffic than the rest of the British waterway network put together. The photograph (fig. 4.52) shows Boulters Lock at Maidenhead on a Whitsun weekend. These locks are seriously congested at busy times. Indeed river use is so

Fig. 4.50 *Typical hotel advertisement. Why does the hotel have its own section of river?*

Ye Complete Angler Portland

Privately owned and managed hotel set in large garden with private fishing on own trout stream and access to both Shannon and Lough Derg fisheries. All bedrooms with private bath or shower, colour TV, direct dial telephone, central heating throughout. Special fishing weekends and events. Tutors and Beginners' courses available.

Fig. 4.52 *Boulters Lock on the river Thames. Why do you think the Thames is so popular?*

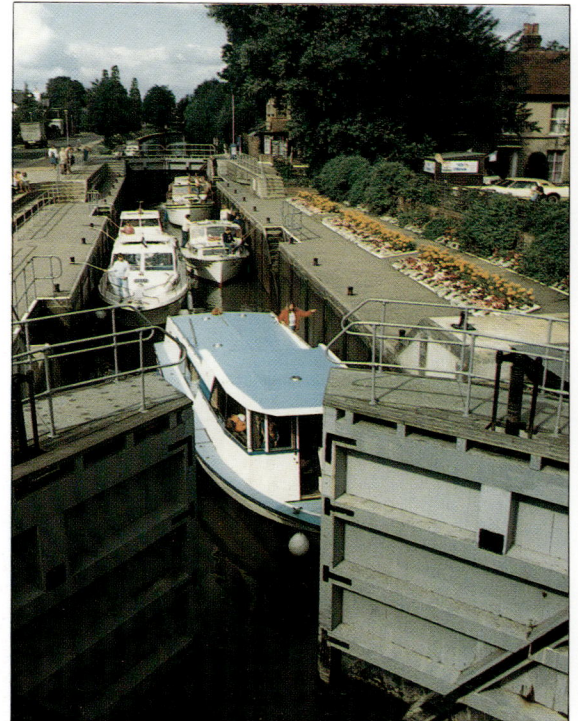

Fig. 4.53 *Estuary activities, Southampton docks. Suggest some possible conflicts and problems. How would you try to solve them?*

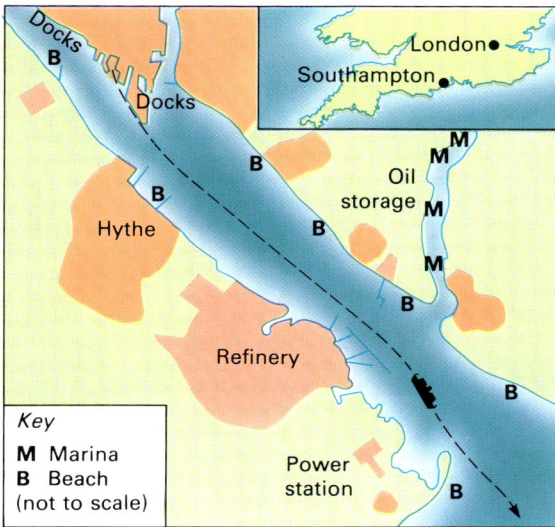

Key
M Marina
B Beach
(not to scale)

great that erosion of the banks, by waves from the boats, is as big a problem as pollution. The tidal sections of the river are extensively used for sailing and windsurfing. This activity may lead to conflict with some of the other estuary activities, as is indicated in the map (fig. 4.53).

Tourism

Rivers are major tourist attractions. They can offer spectacular views of wooded gorges, as along the Wye on the Wales–England border. Sometimes rivers simply offer cool water for paddling and swimming. Many urban parks are arranged around rivers or streams. The River Lea, on the eastern edge of London, has been turned into a long linear park by the Lee Valley Regional Park Authority. This is an example of managing a river for recreational needs. The total area of the park is 4000 ha following the course of the River Lea for 37 km.

There are thirty-nine river channels and about 100 lakes (chiefly flooded gravel pits) which together cover 1020 ha. In 1966, the Lee Valley Regional Park Authority was set up. At the time the area was a mess of old gravel pits and declining market gardens. Today over 2 million visitors use the new facilities and 8–9 million visit the open spaces each year. Figure 4.54 shows some of the facilities that have been built.

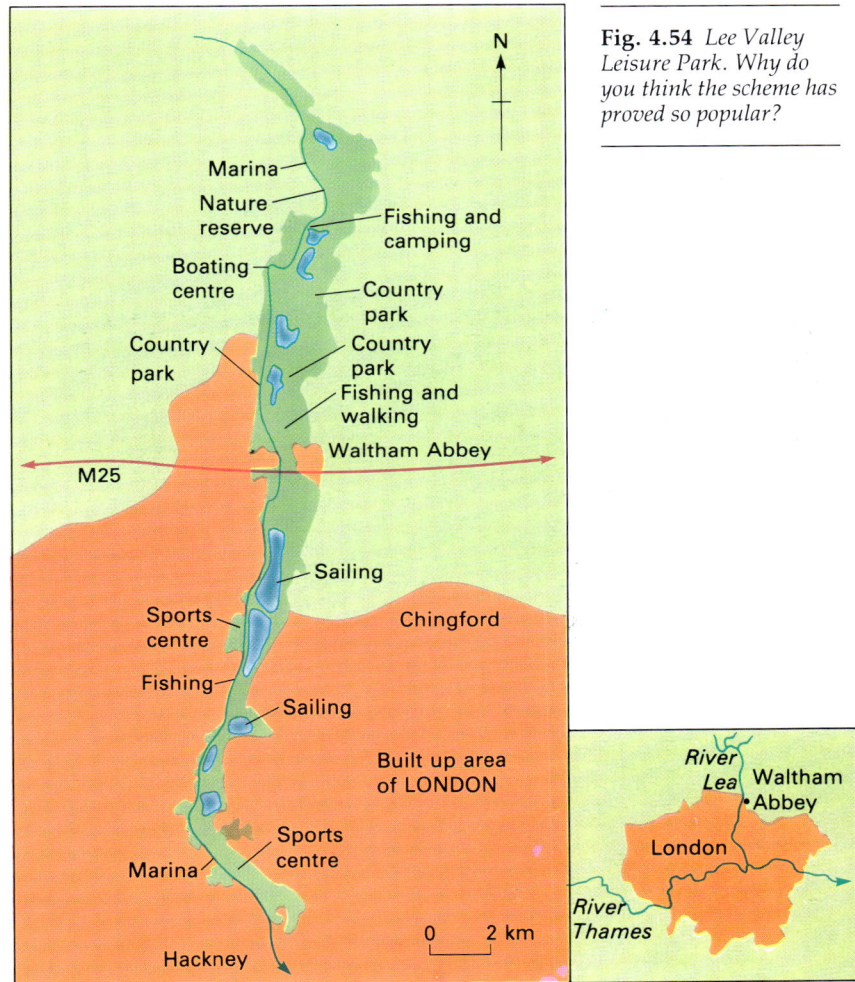

Fig. 4.54 *Lee Valley Leisure Park. Why do you think the scheme has proved so popular?*

Activities

Look at fig. 4.54.
1 Devise a way of classifying the Lee Valley activities. Draw a diagram to show the number of activities in each of your chosen groups. Why is there such a variety of activities?
2 Future proposals include a water-sports centre, fieldstudy centre, golf centre and a motor-cycling area. For each of these proposals suggest the advantages and disadvantages to the area and to existing activities.
3 Why do such activities need to be managed and who might object?

5 ICE IMPACTS

Glacial erosion

In areas of cold climate ice is a major factor in the landscape, as shown on the map (fig. 5.1). The largest ice sheet today is Antarctica but ice can even be found on the equator in high mountainous areas.

In the past these ice sheets have spread over vast areas, causing an ice age. This happened to Europe many times. As the temperatures fell the ice began to move down from the highlands by slipping and sliding. Tongues of ice moved down the existing river valleys. These are called glaciers. Ice is a semi-solid and so only flows slowly over and around areas. It can wear away or erode in a number of ways.

Fig. 5.1 *The areas of ice today. Why do the poles have so much ice?*

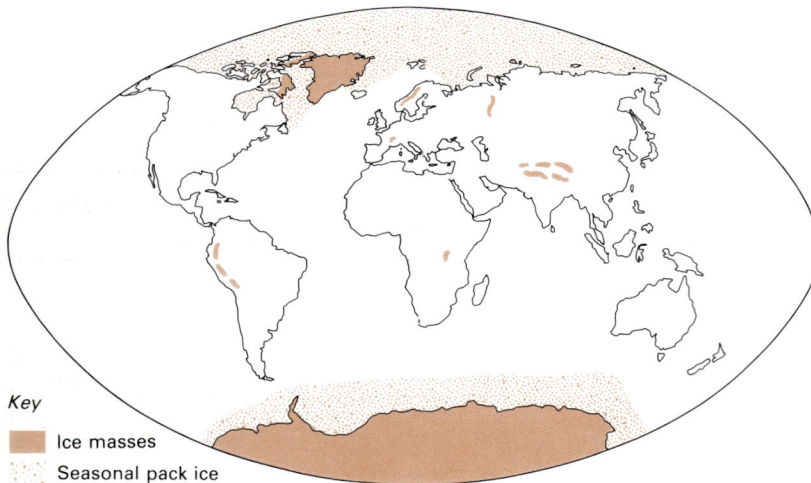

Key
■ Ice masses
░ Seasonal pack ice

Fig. 5.2 *Rock scratches. Which way was the glacier moving?*

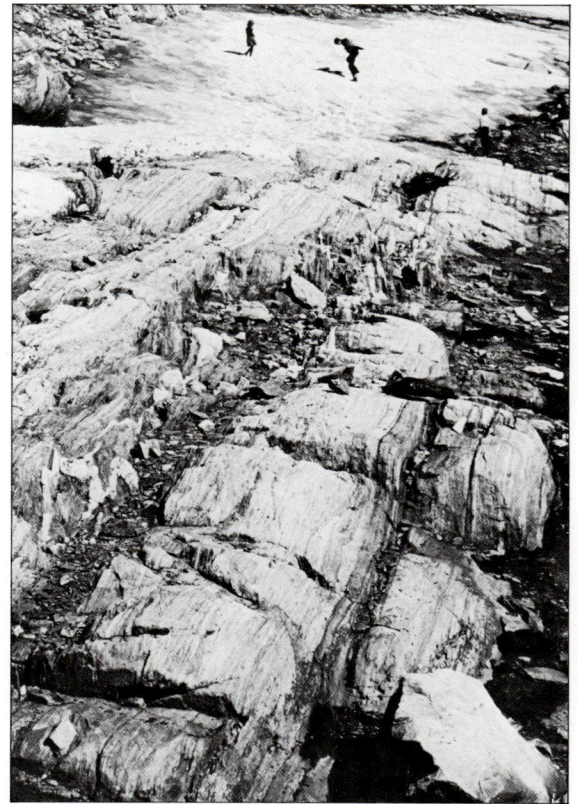

Types of erosion

1 The sheer weight of ice may crush the underlying rock. The Greenland ice cap is over 3000 m thick in places and so must exert a great weight on the landscape.
2 Debris in the base of ice may scratch across the rocks as the ice moves. The photograph (fig. 5.2) shows such scratches or striations.

Their direction indicates the direction of ice movement. They are rarely very long as the debris is either crushed to bits or forced up into the ice.
3 Melting ice may get into cracks or joints and freeze again, so pushing out blocks of rock.
4 The ice can freeze onto loose blocks and then pull them off as it moves down the valley.
5 The ice bulldozes along already shattered rocks. Rocks near the ice may be very broken up by perma-frost activity.

The rate of erosion

This depends on a number of factors as shown in fig. 5.3. If snowfall increases then the ice will become more likely to erode. Sometimes the base of the valley differs in hardness of rock and so some areas are more easily eroded. These eroded basins may later form lakes such as Thirlmere in the Lake District (shown in fig. 5.4). These are often called finger lakes. Originally Thirlmere was a number of smaller lakes but the basin was artificially dammed and a larger lake created. Some of these basin lakes are very deep. Loch Ness is one of the deepest, averaging 130 m.

Human activity

Glacial erosion can aid human activity. As the glaciers grind through the valleys they steepen the sides and sweep away any top soil. This has helped both mining and quarrying in areas such as North Wales by exposing seams of minerals and rocks. Slate, copper, iron, lead and gold have all been mined in the area. Extensive slate quarries and mines still operate in areas such as Blaneau Ffestiniog but several have become tourist attractions. Many of these mines closed in the early twentieth century including those on the slopes of Snowdon. Today there is renewed interest in these mines as world prices rise. Glacial erosion may also help humans by eroding valleys and passes through such mountainous barriers as the Alps and Himalayas. People have completed the work of the ice by building tunnels through mountain barriers.

Fig. 5.3 *Factors controlling the rate of erosion*

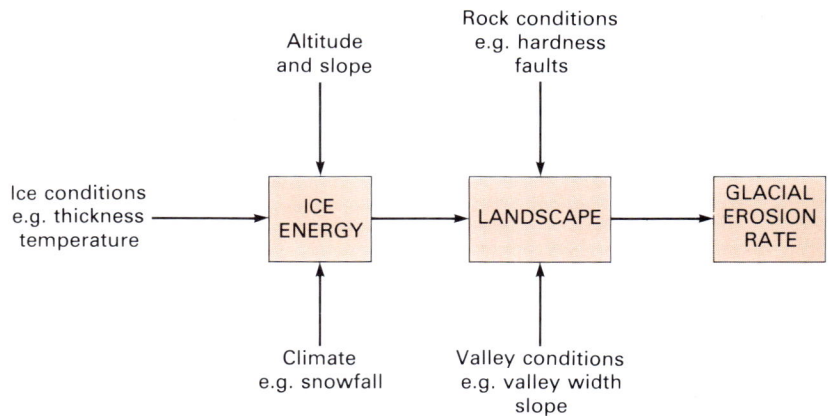

Fig. 5.4 *Thirlmere. Why are lakes like this often called finger lakes? Why was this larger lake created by the damming?*

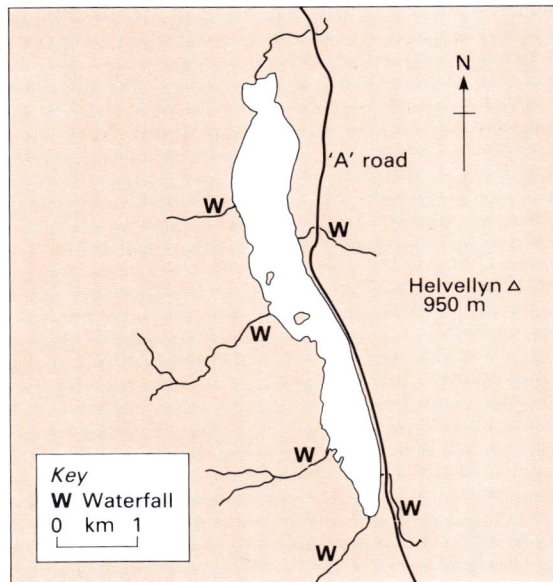

Fig. 5.5 *Two glaciated valleys*

Activities

1 Look at the field sketches (fig. 5.5). Both show valleys that have been eroded by ice.Make a list of differences between the two valleys. Why do you think they might have these differences?

2 Find an Ordnance Survey map of either North Wales or Highland Scotland. Measure the width of the glaciated valleys. Draw a scatter diagram to show these widths. What pattern do you find?

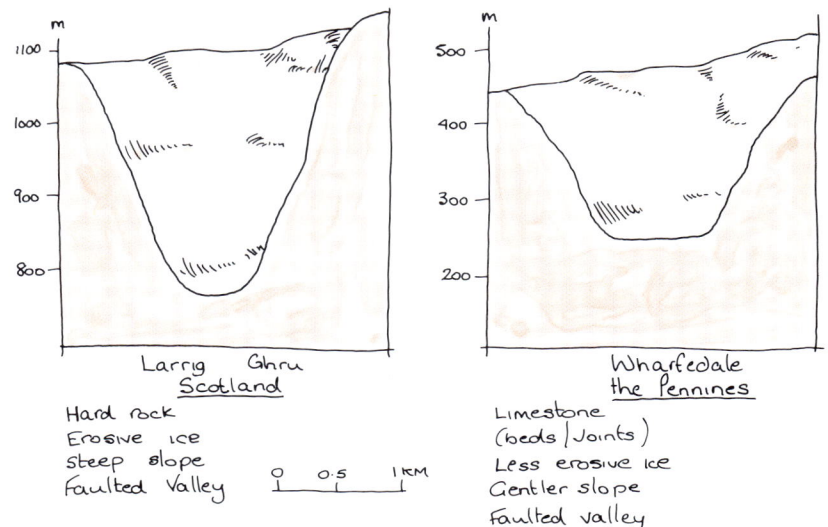

Larrig Ghru
Scotland

Hard rock
Erosive ice
steep slope
Faulted Valley

Wharfedale
the Pennines

Limestone
(beds/Joints)
Less erosive ice
Gentler slope
Faulted valley

Glaciers and relief

Valleys

Unlike a river, a glacier will fill a valley and so erode both the bed and sides, as shown in fig. 5.6. The glacier follows old river valleys because they are lower and so it grinds the V-shape of the river valley into a steep U-shape.

Fig. 5.6 *The making of a U-shaped valley. What do you think controls the exact shape of the U?*

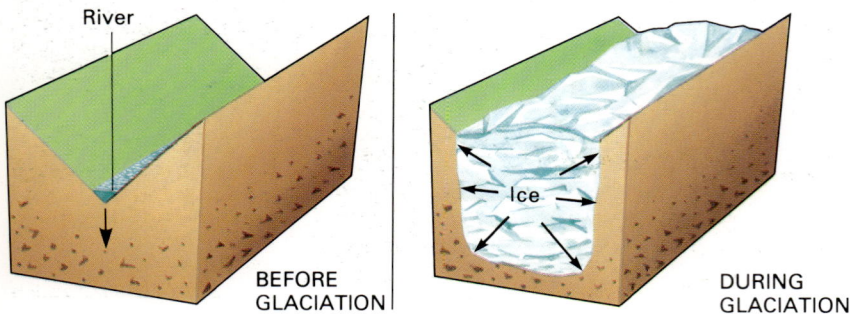

Fig. 5.8 *Kilnsey crag*

As the ice does not easily follow the bends of a river valley it tends to erode a very straight-sided valley. Look at fig. 5.7 and the photograph (fig. 5.8). The valley is not only wider at Kilnsey but its side has also been undercut there, forming a spectacular crag. The ice deepens the main valley more than a smaller tributary valley. This valley is left

Fig. 5.7 *Plan of the valley at Kilnsey*

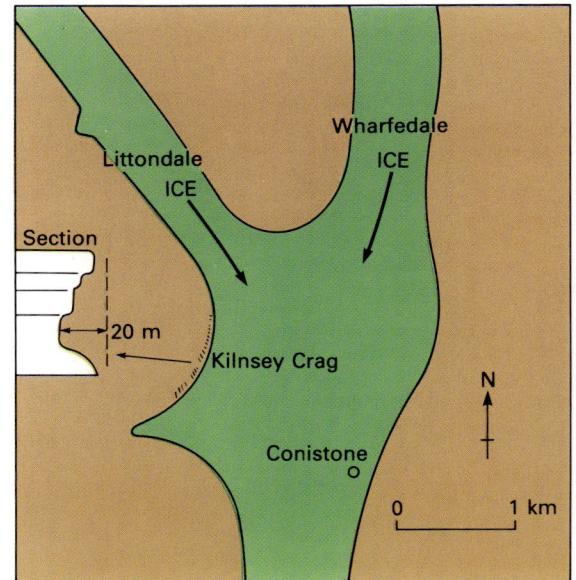

'hanging', with a much steeper junction with the main valley, as shown in fig. 5.9. When the rivers begin to flow again after the ice age, a waterfall forms which may deposit a fan of debris at its base.

Fig. 5.9 *The making of a hanging valley. What economic benefit might these hanging valleys provide?*

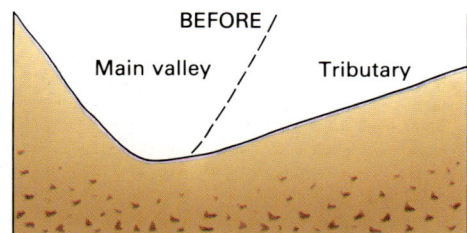

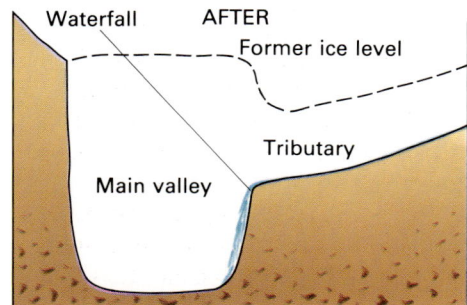

Corries

Hollows high on the mountain side will collect snow in winter. The snow melts during the day, or in summer, and freezes at night. This freezing and thawing breaks up the underlying rock and so deepens the hollow. This is called a nivation hollow. As it gets deeper the snow collects enough to turn into ice. This ice tends to rotate and slip, as shown in fig. 5.11. As it slips, stones and dirt at the base grind the hollow deeper and steeper. Why is a 'lip' of solid rock left? When the ice melts this lip acts as a dam to form a small lake called a tarn. This hollow, as shown in the photograph (fig. 5.12), is called a corrie or cwm or cirque.

Fig. 5.10 *Pattern of corries in North Wales*

| Direction | Corrie directions | |
	Snowdon	Glyders
NE	7	11
SE	1	0
SW	2	0
NW	4	3
	14	14

Fig. 5.11 *Erosion by a corrie glacier*

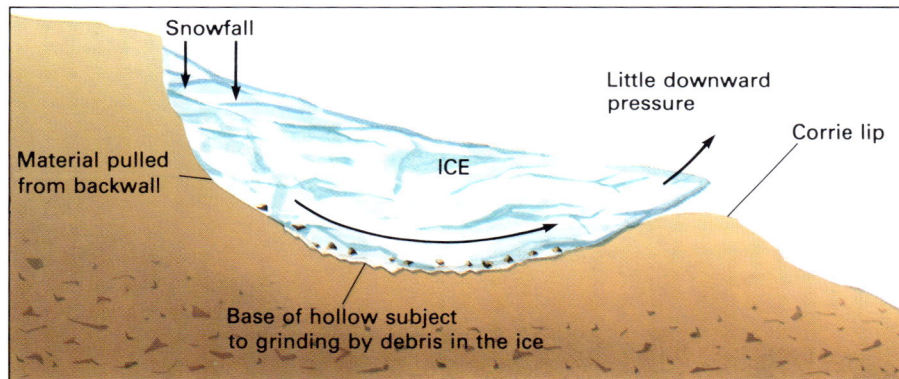

Activities

1 Look at table 5.10. Compare this pattern against the pattern that would have come about by chance, when we might expect each direction to have 25% of the corries. How does this compare with the observed pattern? Why is there a difference?
2 How might the pattern differ in New Zealand?

Fig. 5.12 *A typical corrie*

Fig. 5.13 *An arête and pyramidal peak*

Arêtes and peaks

As corries are eroded and become larger, so the area of rock between them is reduced in size until it becomes a steep-sided thin ridge called an arête, as shown in the photograph (fig. 5.13). If corries form on many sides of a high peak then the entire summit is steepened and eroded away to produce a pyramidal peak. Snowdon is such a peak. Such peaks are uncommon in Britain as this needs high areas of relief. Can you discover any other famous pyramidal peaks?

Glacial streamlining

Fig. 5.14 *Plan of a drumlin. Why does this shape offer least resistance to the ice?*

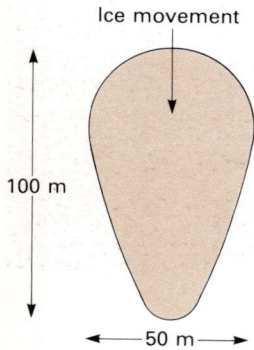

Whatever material ice passes over it tends to mould and streamline it in order to reduce friction.

Drumlins

These are streamlined mounds of soft glacial deposits, as shown in fig. 5.14. As the ice passes over thick areas of deposits they are squeezed into the shape that offers least resistance. They occur in areas where the ice is confined and the pressure of ice is great. The greater the pressure the more the drumlin becomes shaped like a tear drop. They may also be formed when debris collects around rocks, which act as coves and slow down the ice.

The field sketch (fig. 5.15) shows an area of drumlins in the Ribblesdale district of the Pennines. Their blunt ends face towards the direction of ice advance to increase the streamlining. The river now has to flow around these obstacles.

Roche Moutonnée

If the ice passes over a hard-rock outcrop it will streamline it. Figure 5.16 shows a field sketch of a rock landform known as a roche moutonnée near Malham Tarn in the Pennines. The side nearest the ice was smoothed, polished and worn down by the force of the ice pushing against the outcrop. The far side was plucked and quarried by the ice as it pulled away from the outcrop.

Fig. 5.15 *Field sketch of drumlins in Ribblesdale. Why do drumlins create problems for transport and farming?*

Fig. 5.16 *Roche moutonnée, Tennant Gill near Malham Tarn*

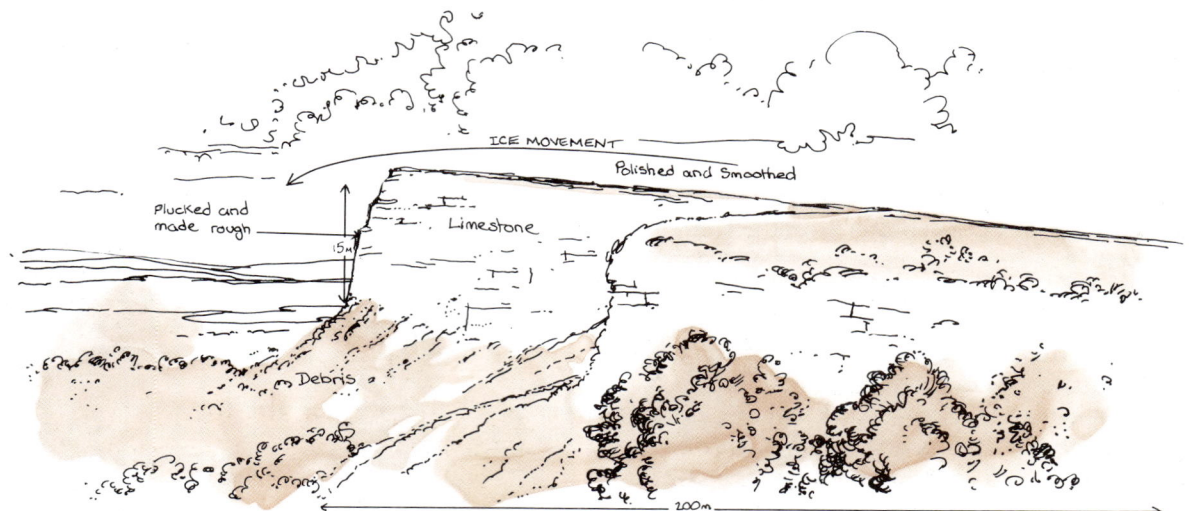

Glacial transport

Erratics

Much of the material deposited in glaciated areas has come a considerable distance. The exact distance and direction is shown by the size and type of debris. Look at the photograph (fig. 5.17) of some of the Norber rocks above Austwick in the Pennines. Many weigh 2–3 tonnes. These do not match the underlying type of rock, which is limestone, so they are called erratics. Their large size and angular shape suggest that they have not been transported far. They were probably pushed up from much lower down in the valley.

Fig. 5.17 *The Norber rocks, Austwick. How do you think the ice can pick up and carry such material?*

Fig. 5.18 *Norfolk tills*

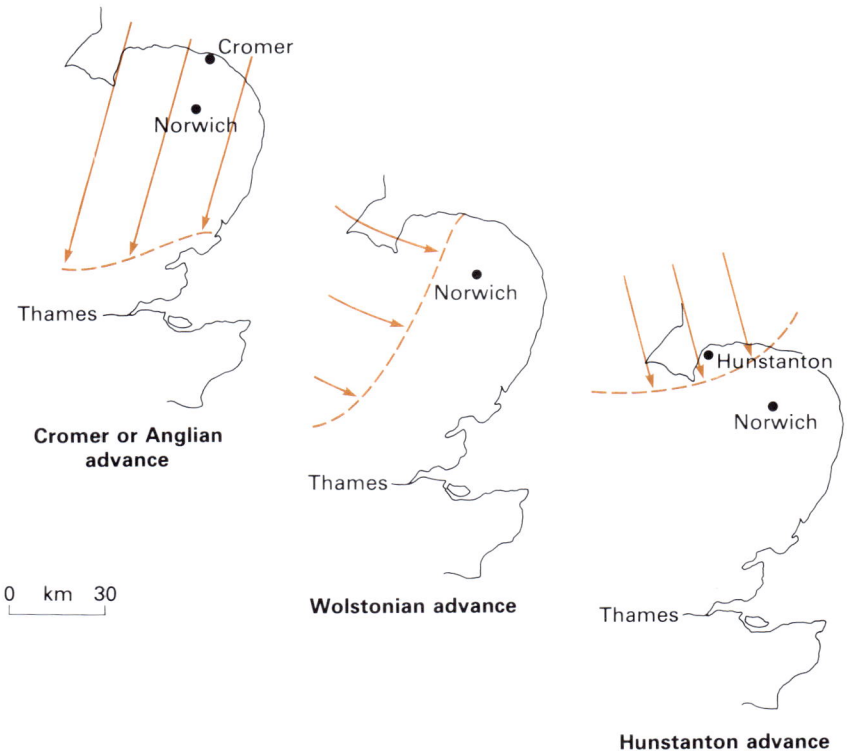

Cromer
Norwich
Thames
Cromer or Anglian advance

Norwich
Thames
Wolstonian advance

Hunstanton
Norwich
Thames
Hunstanton advance

0   km   30

Boulder clay (till)

Not all erratics are large. Two of the main materials carried by the ice are fine dirt and stones. When the ice melts these are left as deposits called till or boulder clay. Even these deposits tell us a lot about the direction of ice movement.
This till may fill in the existing river valleys if it is thick enough. In Norfolk, the pre-glacial rivers flowed from south to north, but today they do not!

Fig. 5.19 *An analysis of a sample of Cromer till*

Crushed chalk	22%
Rounded flints	37%
Silts and sands	30%
Sea shells	8%
Metamorphic rocks	3%

Activities

1 The map (fig. 5.18) shows the various deposits in Norfolk. How would you test them for evidence of their age and direction?
2 Table 5.19 shows an analysis of a sample of Cromer till. Draw a diagram to show the local and erratic material. What is the evidence to suggest that the till might have crossed the North Sea from Norway?

Glacial deposits

The edges of glaciers become very dirty with material eroded from the valley sides and fallen from the highland above. Some is bulldozed along by the ice. The typical dirtiness of the end of a glacier is shown in the photograph (fig. 5.20). When the ice melts this dirt is deposited.

Fig. 5.20 *Dirty ice margin*

DURING
Lateral moraines

AFTER
Lateral moraines

Ice

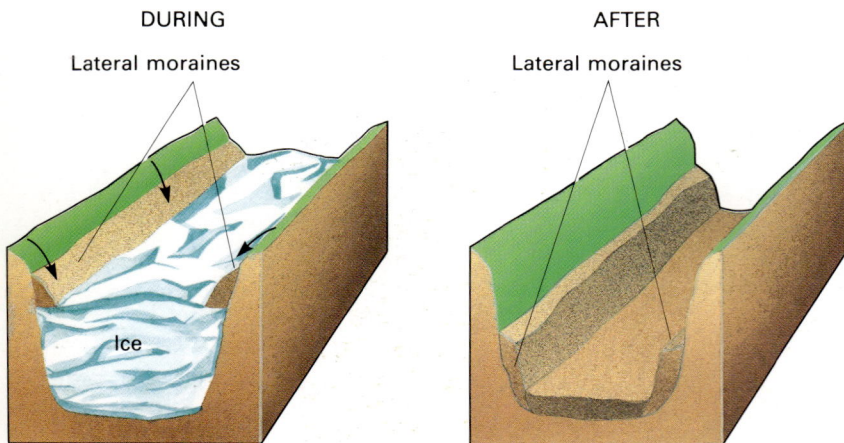

Fig. 5.21 *Lateral moraine formation. Why does ice melt at glacier edges? Can you suggest any ways in which these deposits could help human activity?*

Upland areas

The ice tends to melt at the valley edges. Any dirt that collects at the edges is left there as a lateral moraine, as shown in fig. 5.21, when the ice melts.

If two or more valleys join, then the lateral moraines may merge to form a central, or medial, moraine. Figure 5.22 shows the various moraines in Wharfedale.

The terminal moraines are formed at the end of the glacier as the ice bulldozes along loose material. Wharfedale has at least three terminal moraines in its upper stretches,

Fig. 5.22 *Wharfedale moraines. Why is the medial moraine so short and bent?*

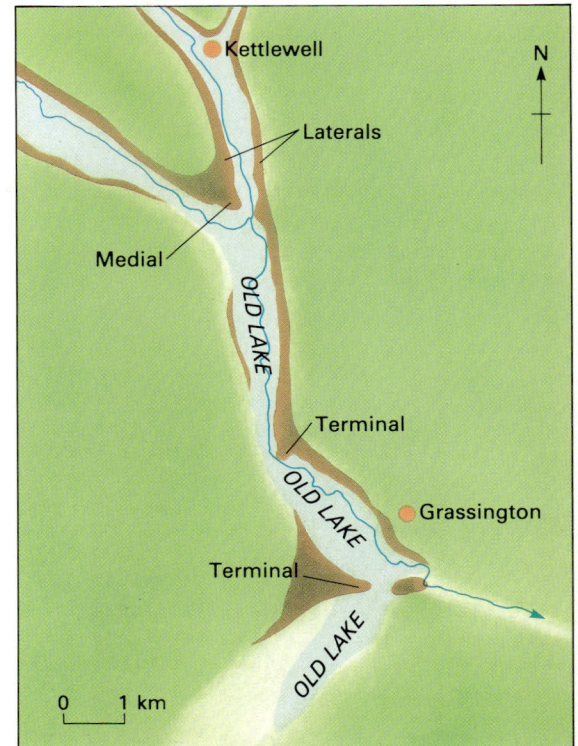

suggesting several ice re-advances. The photograph (fig. 5.23) shows a typical terminal moraine at Llyn Idwal in North Wales. Like the ones in Wharfedale, it acted as a dam to create lakes. What evidence would you look for to prove that lakes once existed in the valley?

Fig. 5.23 *Terminal moraine, Llyn Idwal*

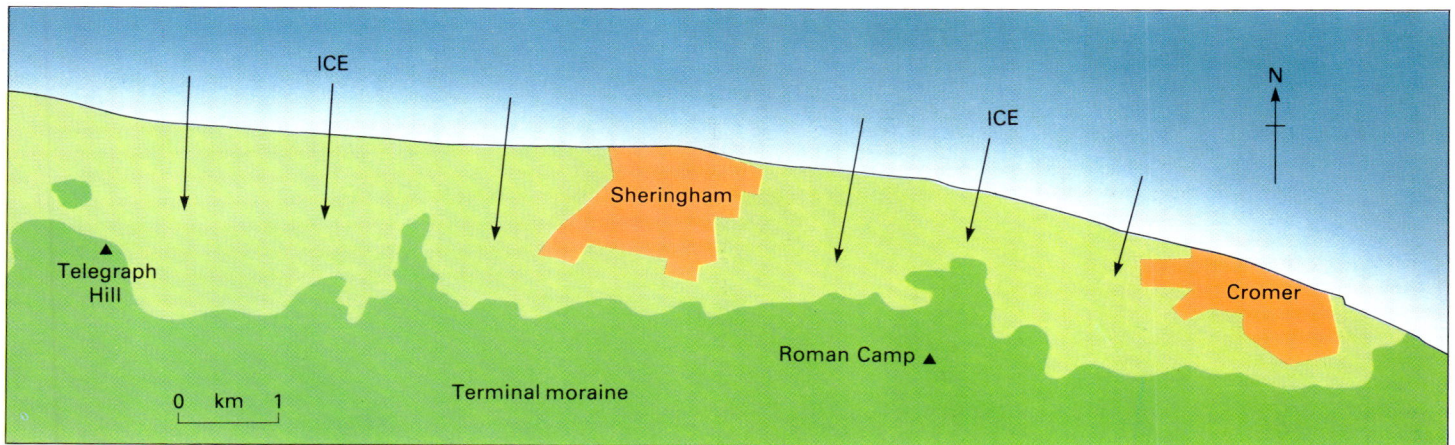

Fig. 5.24 *Holt–Cromer ridge, north Norfolk*

Lowland areas

When a glacier spreads out into a lowland area, it may begin to melt and material might be deposited. One of the largest terminal moraines in Britain is the Holt–Cromer ridge, in Norfolk, shown in fig. 5.24. It is over 15 km long and is probably 2 km wide. It rises to 100 m at Roman Camp, south-west of Cromer.

Fig. 5.25 *View of Holt–Cromer moraine, looking east*

Activities

1 State what evidence you would look for to suggest the direction of ice movement that formed this Holt–Cromer moraine.
2 Explain why no lateral or medial moraines are deposited.
3 Suggest why the moraine might have gained the bend at the western end and explain its wavy (lobate) plan.
4 Look at the photograph (fig. 5.25) which shows the north face of the Holt–Cromer ridge. Draw a fieldsketch of the view and label it using information from the map. What effect does it have on the settlement and land use in the area?

Glacial lakes

There are a variety of lakes in glacial uplands. They differ in size, depth and shape, from small corrie tarns to long 'finger lakes'. They have many uses of local and national importance.

Water storage

The Lake District, Wales and the Pennines have numerous lakes that have been created in U-shaped valleys. Some are natural and some have been created by the local Water Authority. Figure 5.26 shows some of the main reservoirs in Wales. Water is transferred by pipeline or river to meet the large industrial and urban demands of Merseyside and Birmingham. Lake Vyrnwy was created in 1889 by damming a glaciated valley. The flooding of the valley led to the drowning of the village Llanwddyn under 60 million m^3 of water.

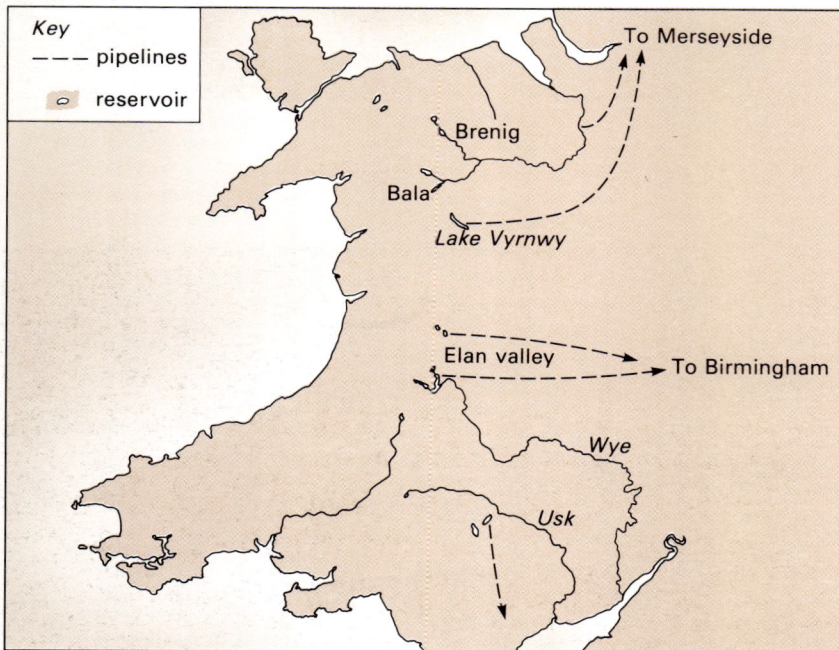

Fig. 5.26 *Main reservoirs in Wales*

Tourism

Lakes provide a variety of uses for tourists, and can bring economic benefits as well as environmental damage to the lake's area.

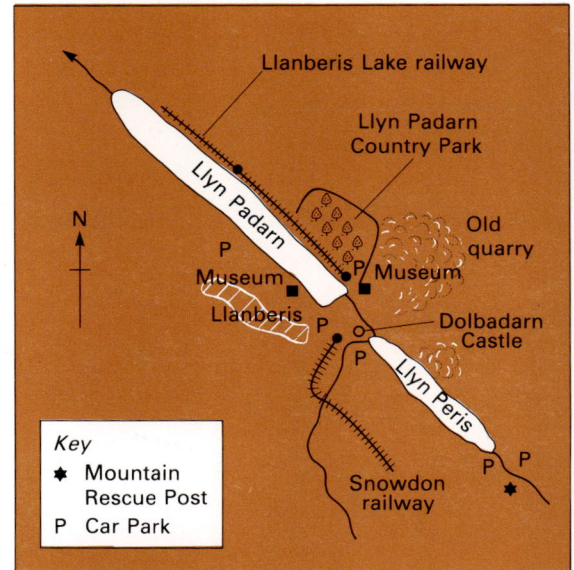

Fig. 5.27 *Northern part of Llanberis valley*

Power generation

The areas of steep slopes, natural lakes, high rainfall and low evaporation rates are ideal for the production of hydroelectricity. Hydroelectricity makes up 7% of British power production and these plants are concentrated in glaciated areas like North Wales. Figures 5.28 and 5.29 show the situation and site of the

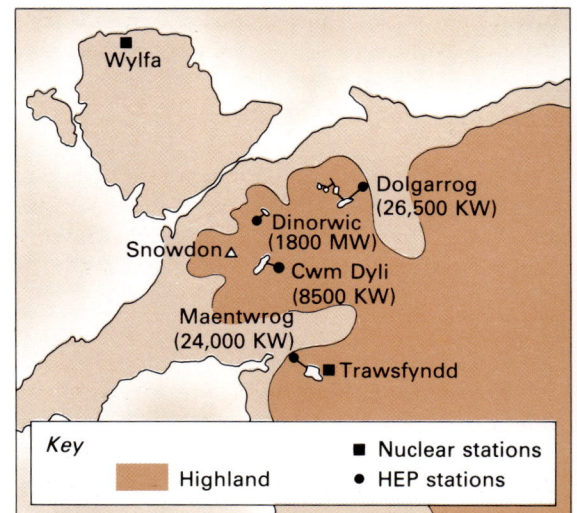

Fig. 5.28 *Power sites in North Wales*

Activities

Look at fig. 5.27 which shows part of the Llanberis valley in North Wales.

1 Classify the attractions of this location, for tourists, into natural and artificial. What is the relative proportion of each group?

2 List the advantages and disadvantages that tourism might bring to the area.

3 Why do restrictions need to be placed on speedboats and water skiing in these lakes?

Dinorwic pump storage scheme in Llanberis valley, North Wales. This is the largest scheme in Britain and uses six turbines to produce 1800 MW. Water is pumped up at night into a glacial lake using spare power. In this case it comes from the nearby nuclear power station at Trawsfyndd. The water is then ready in the morning, in the upper lake, to be sent down the large pipes to turn the turbines and so produce electricity. The upper lake flows down into the lower glacial lake where it is stored until it can be pumped back up again the next night. The whole works is concealed underground in an old slate mine to reduce environmental impact on this scenic area. Sometimes such local hydroelectric schemes have attracted power-thirsty industries like pulp mills, and at Fort William in Scotland there is an aluminium smelter. Power costs make up more than 20% of the cost of making aluminium so a location near a cheap, renewable and large source of energy is attractive. Suggest why such industries have not moved near the Welsh power plants.

Farming

Often glacial lakes dry up, or are filled in by silt and deltas. As they dry they create very fertile farmland. The photograph (fig. 5.30) shows part of an old lake floor in a glaciated area.

Other uses

These include fishing and transport, which are major uses of glacial lakes in developing countries such as Peru. Why do you think these uses of glacial lakes are not as important in Britain?

Fig. 5.29 *Site of Dinorwic hydroelectric power station*

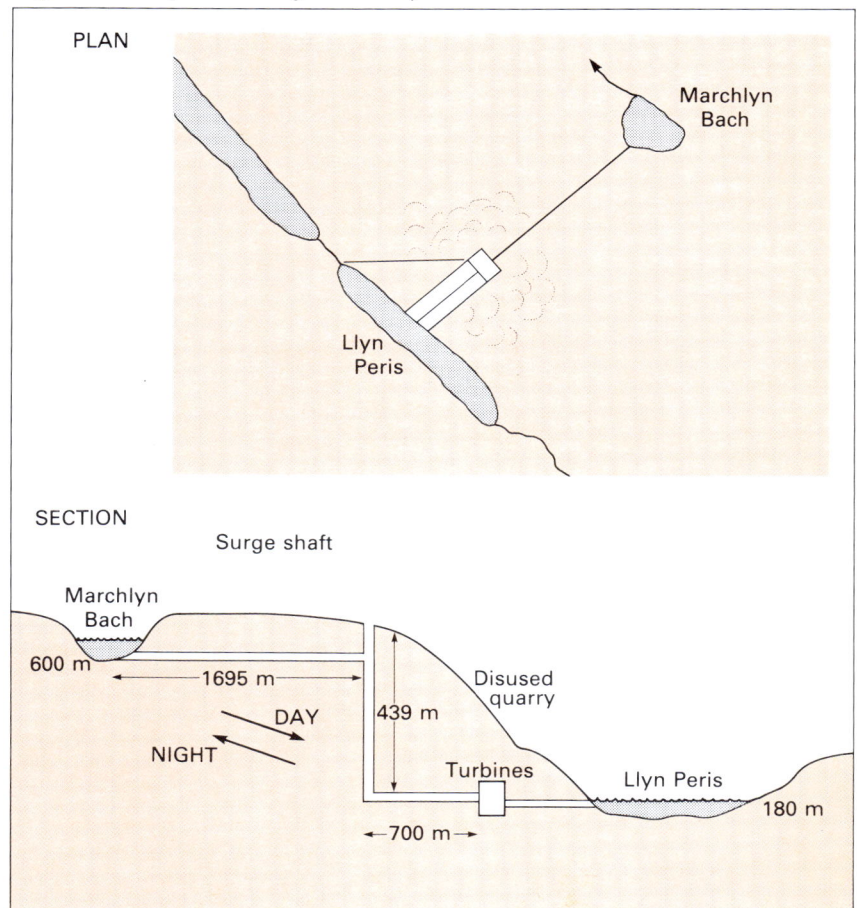

Fig. 5.30 *Former glacial lake. Draw a sketch across the valley and label the main types of farming shown. Why is it rare to find crops in such valleys?*

Meltwater erosion and deposition

As the ice melts, water becomes an important factor.

Erosion

If the water carries little debris, or is in large volumes, it may erode the landscape. Water may flow off the ice and the valley side and erode a vertical chute between the ice and valley side, as shown in the photograph (fig. 5.31).

Fig. 5.31 *Chute at Kilnsey Crag. Why don't all the chutes reach the valley floor?*

In lowland areas meltwater may flow into river valleys, making them deeper. A typical example of this is the Tyne and Wear, as shown in fig. 5.32. Suggest what opportunities and problems such a deepening of the river might have created for human activity.

Fig. 5.32 *Tyne and Wear valleys*

Deposition

1 *Eskers*   As the water slows down, or becomes overloaded with debris, it may be forced to deposit its load. Sometimes it is deposited in the form of a gravel ridge called an esker, which is the old bed of one of these streams.

Fig. 5.33 *The Blakeney esker*

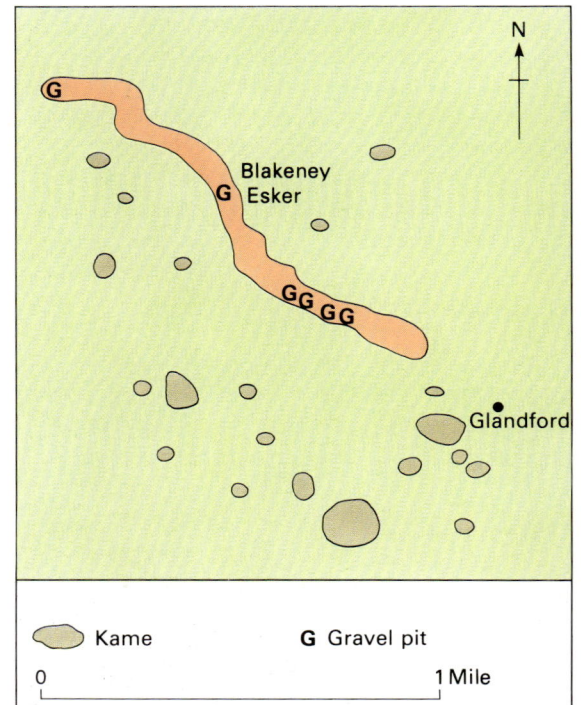

Activities

The Blakeney esker in Norfolk is shown in fig. 5.33.
1 Study fig. 5.33 and present, with evidence, an explanation of the plan of the esker.
2 The photograph (fig. 5.34) shows a section of the esker. Draw a fieldsketch of the scene. Add on a scale to show the height and width of the section. How deep is the soil layer?
3 What effect has this deposit had on the uses of the land by humans?

Fig. 5.34 *A section through the Blakeney esker*

These meltwater features are always bedded, with the beds representing fine sediment dropped in winter and coarse stones dropped during the heavy spring and summer melt.
2   *Kames*   In some cases meltwater falls through holes in the melting ice, as shown in fig. 5.35. As it hits the bottom, the water loses energy and so deposits a fan of debris called a kame. When the ice melts these are left as conical hills, as shown in the photograph (fig. 5.36) taken in Norfolk.

Fig. 5.35 *The formation of kames*

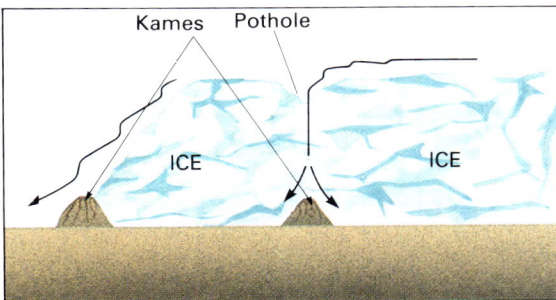

Fig. 5.36 *Norfolk kames. What effect do these hills have on farming?*

Fig. 5.37 *Kame terrace formation. What other glacial deposits do kame terraces resemble? How could you tell them apart?*

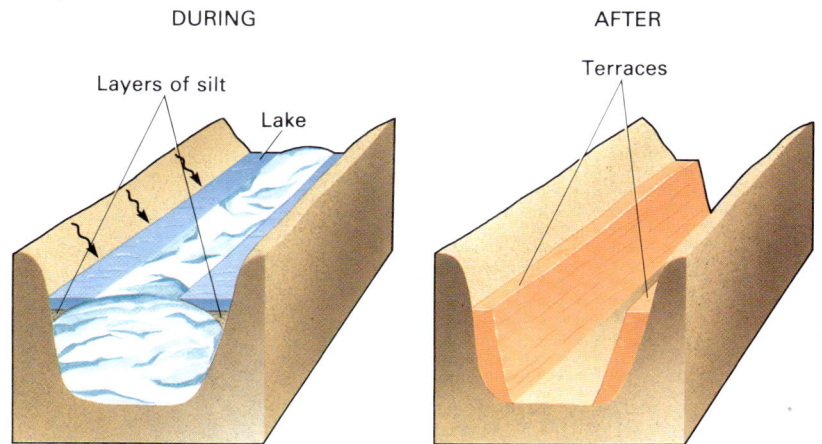

In upland areas these kames can be deposited at the edge of the ice in small lakes. These form because the dark rock absorbs more heat than the shiny ice surface, and then it melts the ice immediately next to it, as shown in fig. 5.37. When the ice melts away these are left as terraces of bedded material called kame terraces.
3   *Outwash plains*   As meltwater leaves the front of a melting glacier or ice sheet, it forms a series of streams that form braids across the area. These create large deposits of outwash sands and gravels. As the water slows down and loses energy it deposits the largest, heaviest load near the ice front. Finer sands and silts may be carried away for some distance. Figure 5.38 shows typical outwash deposits.

Fig. 5.38 *Outwash deposits.*

Fjords and economic opportunities

As glaciers erode down they produce deep valleys. If the valleys occur on the coast, they maybe drowned as the sea-level rises when the ice sheets melt. This produces deep, straight, coastal inlets called fjords, (fig. 5.39).

Fig. 5.39 *Sogne Fjord, Norway*

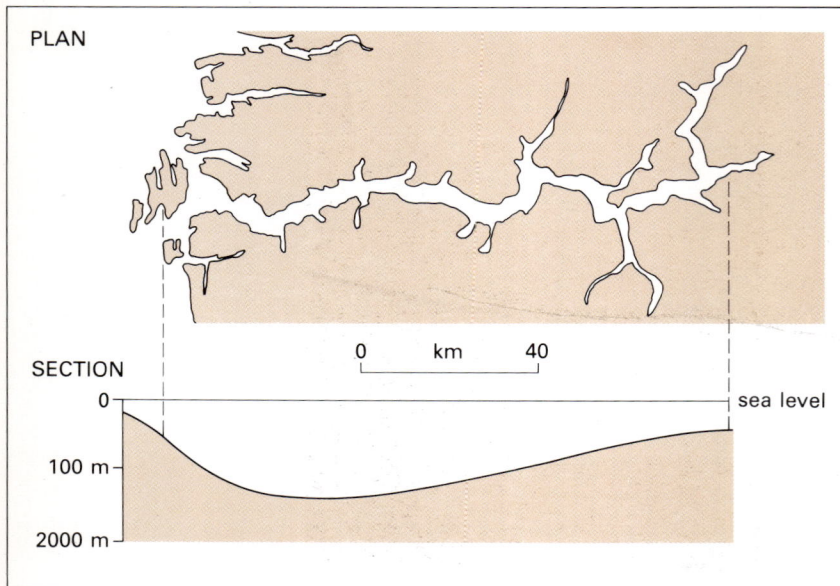

As the ice melted at the end of the Ice Age, a great deal of weight was removed from the land. The land began to rise slowly. As it rose it took various beach features with it. Look at the field sketch (fig. 5.40), sketched near Oban in Scotland. Raised beaches are very important in the fjord regions because they are one of the few areas of flat land.

Deepwater ports

Look at the map (fig. 5.41) of Loch Long on the west coast of Scotland, which is now a deepwater port. Crude oil is unloaded into a

Fig. 5.41 *Loch Long, Scotland. Why was it considered an ideal site for a deep-water port for oil super tankers?*

Fig. 5.40 *Raised beach at Oban, Scotland. What evidence is there to show that the area is a raised beach?*

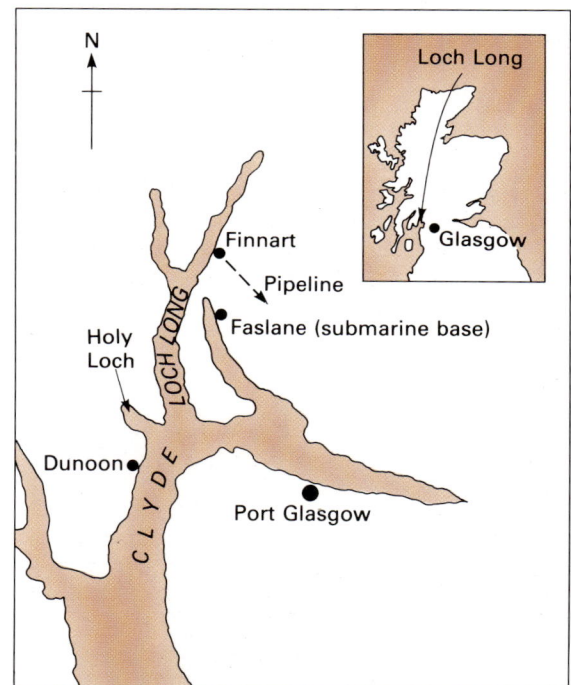

Activities

1 Can you suggest why fjords tend to be so straight?
2 The mouth of a fjord is often very shallow. How much shallower is the mouth of the fjord in fig. 5.39 compared to the deepest part? Why do you think the ice was less erosive by the time it reached the fjord mouth?
3 What effect does this shallow mouth (threshold) have on storm waves entering the fjord?

30 cm diameter pipeline that is 90 km long which takes the oil to the Grangemouth refinery on the east coast of Scotland. Finnart is deep enough to take tankers over 300 000 tonnes with a draught of 30 m. Holy Loch and Faslane are used as naval bases, especially for submarines. Such port activities may threaten the local wildlife, as pollution and noise get trapped in these narrow inlets.

Shipbuilding

In recent years many of these deepwater fjords have been developed, in Scotland and Norway, as oil-rig building sites.

Fishing

These fjords provide ideal sites for fishing ports but the deep sheltered water is also suitable for fish farming. Many Norwegian and Scottish fjords are major sources of trout, salmon and crayfish. Fish farming increases the size and likelihood of survival of valuable species. It is only profitable to farm certain species.

Ferry ports

Figure 5.42 shows a typical Norwegian fjord. Many of the fjords have ports operating a ferry service to the many scattered offshore island communities which have few other links with the outside world.

Tourism

These fjord areas have become important tourist areas in Scotland, New Zealand, British Columbia and Norway.

Fig. 5.42 *Typical Norwegian fjord. Why are ferry ports so important in this kind of area?*

Fig. 5.43 *An advertisement for a fjord holiday*

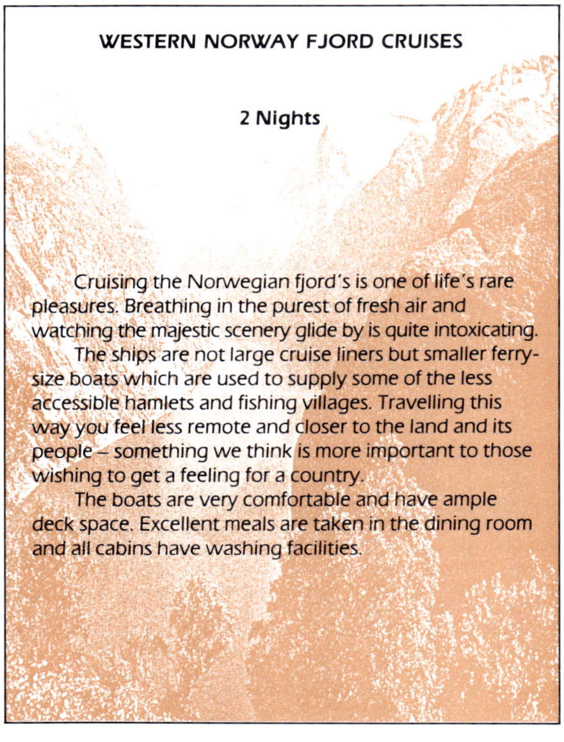

WESTERN NORWAY FJORD CRUISES

2 Nights

Cruising the Norwegian fjord's is one of life's rare pleasures. Breathing in the purest of fresh air and watching the majestic scenery glide by is quite intoxicating.

The ships are not large cruise liners but smaller ferry-size boats which are used to supply some of the less accessible hamlets and fishing villages. Travelling this way you feel less remote and closer to the land and its people – something we think is more important to those wishing to get a feeling for a country.

The boats are very comfortable and have ample deck space. Excellent meals are taken in the dining room and all cabins have washing facilities.

Activities

Read the advertisement for a Norwegian fjord holiday (fig. 5.43).
1 What are the attractions of these cruises? Why do you think 'ferry-size' boats are used?
2 Why has tourism become so important for these remote areas?
3 Try to suggest the attitudes that (a) a fjord villager, and (b) a nature conservationist, might have to increasing tourism in the area.

Glaciated uplands and recreation areas

There is a difference between passive and active tourism. What do the terms mean? Passive includes sight-seeing and sunbathing while active involves physical activity such as climbing, sailing and bird-watching. Upland areas of jagged scenery and rushing rivers attract both types of visitors.

Scotland has four skiing areas, as shown in fig. 5.46. The largest is the Glenshee area, with a capacity of over 14,000 skiers/hour, on four peaks of over 1000 m.

Fig. 5.44 *Glen More ski slopes. What do you think had to be done before the area could be developed for skiing? Why are highlands so suitable for skiing?*

Fig. 5.45 *Glen More Forest Park*

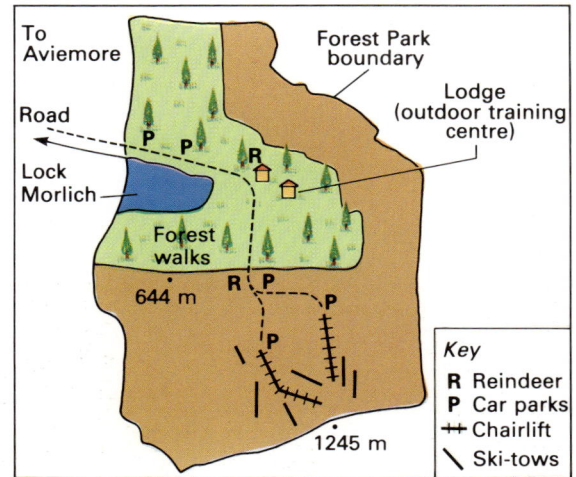

Winter sports

This is a recent trend on the upper glaciated slopes in Scotland, especially in the Cairngorms where in winter over 5000 skiers use the slopes above Aviemore each day, as shown in the photograph (fig. 5.44). In 1974 ski-lifts and tows were built and now there are three chairlifts and seven ski-tows, as shown on the map (fig. 5.45). Aviemore itself has had to develop an all-year-round approach to visitors and has a sports complex including heated swimming-pool, ice-skating rink and a dry ski-slope.

Fig. 5.46 *Scottish ski resorts. Why does Scotland have such limited skiing areas compared with Austria and Switzerland, and why is Scotland trying to develop more areas? Why are resorts like these so rare in the developing world?*

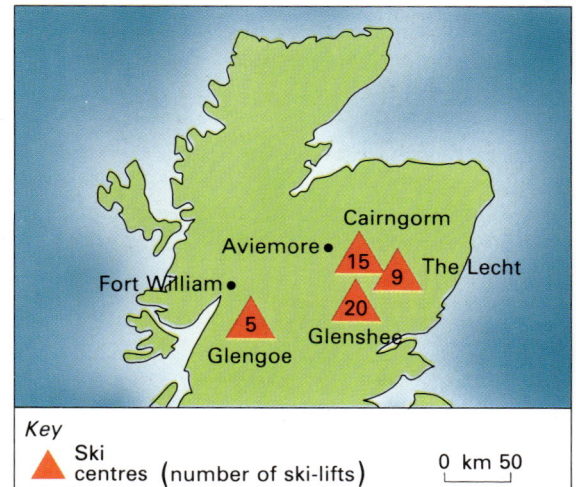

Activities

1 Why does Scotland have such limited skiing areas compared with Austria and Switzerland, and why is Scotland trying to develop more areas?
2 If you were a local villager, how would you feel about these changes to a once lonely and wild area?
3 Why is it risky to let your resort depend purely on attracting people for skiing?

Climbing, hill walking and rambling

These are common activities in glaciated areas because the eroded and frost-shattered landscape provides magnificent open views and difficult climbs, as shown in the photograph (fig. 5.47). There are over ten similar ascents in the Glen More Park, and many of these are rated very difficult. There are many outdoor pursuit centres in these areas with over 140 similar centres in the Snowdonia National Park alone! In recent years there has been a great interest and growth in outdoor pursuits.

Fig. 5.47 *Rock climbing. Why might this sort of activity cause problems?*

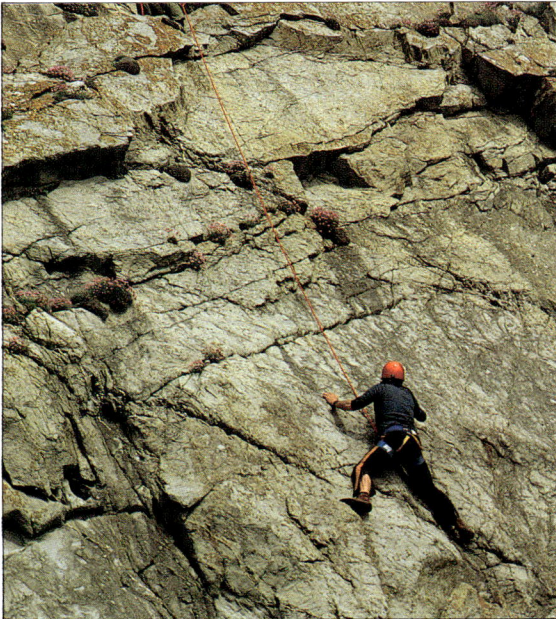

Water sports

Many of the fast streams are used for canoeing and the lakes for sailing.

Nature lovers

These include groups like birdwatchers, amateur geologists, deerstalkers and also reindeer watchers in the case of Glen More, where a herd of seventy to eighty has been established since 1952. Why do the needs of this group conflict with many of the other activities? These conflicts are often difficult to solve and sometimes laws are needed to protect certain wildlife species, like ospreys.

Sightseers

Many people visit these upland areas to see the scenery, visit old castles, tour old mines and quarries, and walk in the many forests. Figure 5.48 shows the visitors to the Llanberis area of North Wales and the acute congestion problems on a summer weekend. Many of these areas are now carefully managed as country parks to reduce the damage to these fragile highland environments (fig. 5.49).

Fig. 5.48 *Visitor survey Llanberis, August 1986*

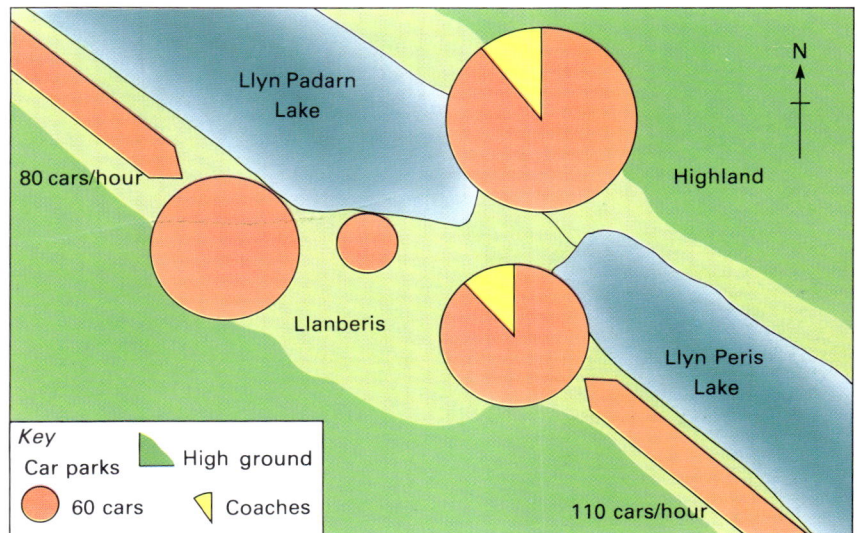

Fig. 5.49 *Lake Padarn Country Park slate quarry*

The uses of glacial deposits

Glacial deposits tend to be sorted into varying sizes of debris by meltwater and wind.

Gravels

These are usually outwash deposits. They drain very quickly and produce only thin acidic soils and so are of little use for farming unless they can be irrigated and fertilised. By adding clay and lime, drainage is slowed and the soil made less acid. Gravels are frequently left as heathland, or planted with conifers to help stabilise the soil and provide commercial forestry. Since 1922, 215 km^2 of the 777 km^2 of the Breckland area of East Anglia have been planted with trees, as shown in fig. 5.50. Scots pines, Corsican pines and Douglas firs have been planted making it the second largest forest in England.

Gravel is frequently quarried for 'ballast' – stones used in building and concrete. Here the sorting of glacial debris is a marked advantage since one quarry can supply a variety of sizes of material, as shown in the photograph (fig. 5.51). Old gravel pits frequently become flooded and form lakes. Many of these infertile gravel areas are now becoming major areas for urban development, because the land is cheap.

Fig. 5.50 *The Breckland. Why do you think this area has been used for army training?*

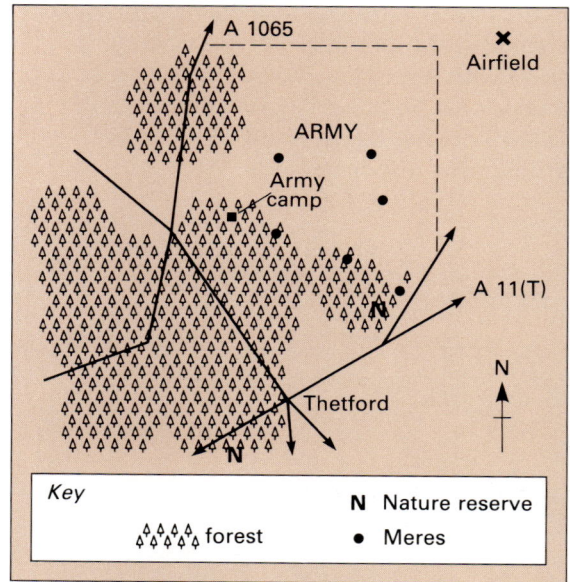

Fig. 5.51 *Quarry, Edgefield Common, Norfolk. What uses do you think there are for different sizes of gravel?*

Fig. 5.52 *Land uses in East Anglia. What are the land uses of the sandy areas? Why do you think airfields are located in areas like these?*

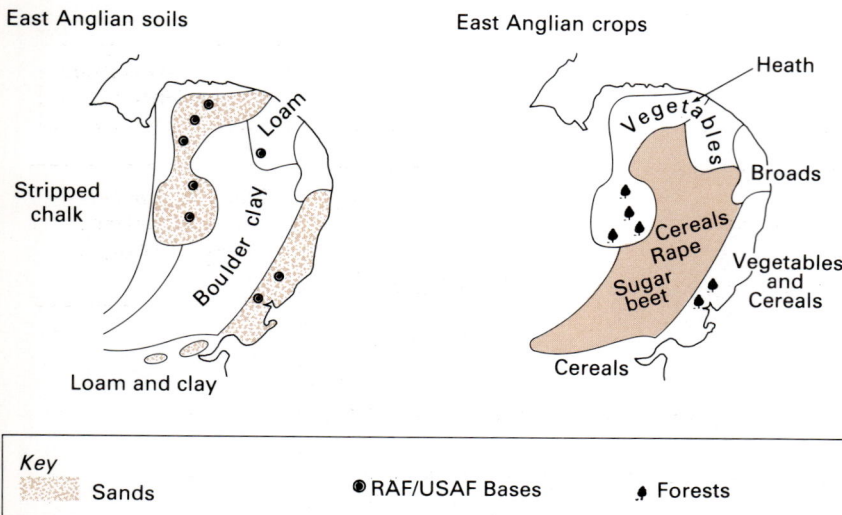

Sands

These are similar to the gravels but are finer and often represent old glacial sand dunes blown along by strong winds. These areas are also infertile and so may be left as heathland. Look at the maps (fig. 5.52) showing land uses in sandy areas. Some of the sands are used in glass making and other industrial processes.

Boulder clay (till)

This deposit varies from very sandy to thick clay. In East Anglia the chalky boulder clay forms very fertile and productive farmland. As the boulder clay is flat, slightly alkaline and well drained, it is ideal for wheat, barley, sugarbeet and rape. On wetter clays, like those in Ireland, dairying and potatoes are more common. Because boulder clay is often deposited unevenly, lakes are common. In Eire these are major sources of recreation, especially sailing and fishing. Many of these lakes formed vast peat bogs. Peat is cut in Eire as a fuel. Eire has nine peat-fired power stations, as shown in the map (fig. 5.53). These provide 20% of the nation's power. The peat is used also as domestic fuel and for gardens. The old peat diggings often become flooded and form lakes. The peat bogs can be very dangerous to careless visitors or animals.

Fig. 5.53 *Glacial deposits in Ireland*

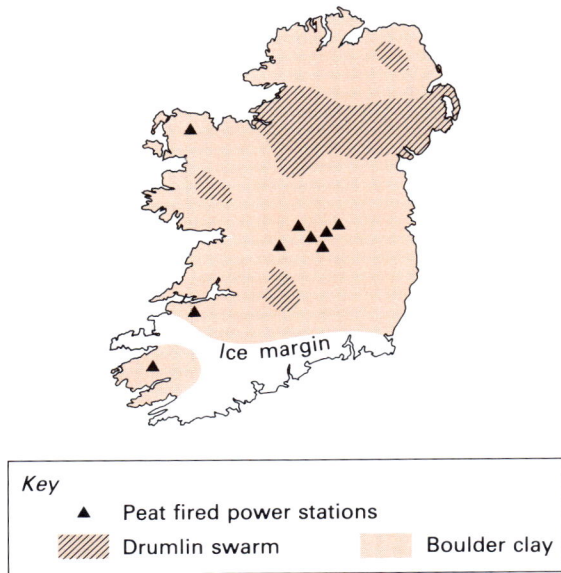

Key
▲ Peat fired power stations
Drumlin swarm   Boulder clay

Loam (loess)

This is fine wind-blown glacial silt and dust that is found on the very edge of glaciated areas. It is a fertile soil compared with gravel. It warms up rapidly in the summer and so is ideal for market gardening and soft-fruit growing. Sometimes this deposit is called brickearth, indicating its other chief use. In south-east Essex a large number of brickworks grew up in the nineteenth century based on local brickearth. Today only two continue to operate in south-east Essex, one of which is shown in the photograph (fig. 5.54).

Fig. 5.54 *Great Wakering Brickworks*

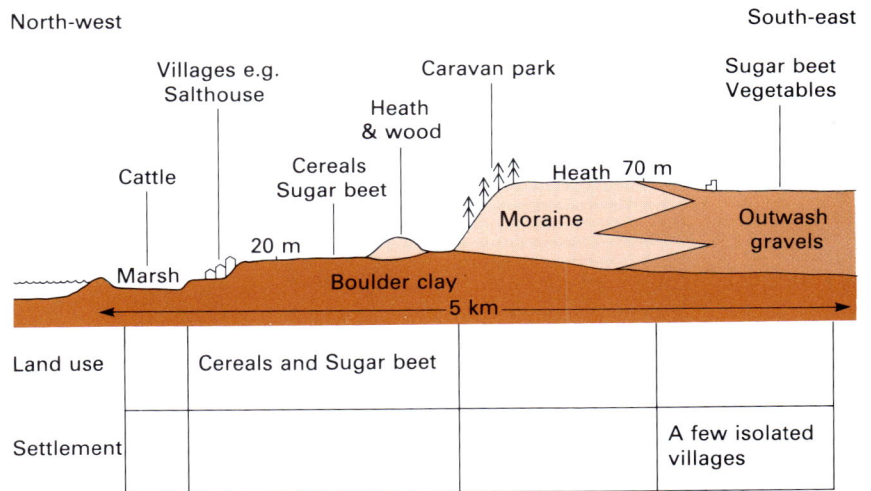

Fig. 5.55 *Land use transect across the Holt–Cromer ridge, Norfolk*

Activities

Look at the land-use transect (fig. 5.55) across the Holt–Cromer moraine in north Norfolk.
1 Complete the transect table.
2 Measure the transect and calculate the percentage of the length occupied by the different land uses. Draw a diagram to show your findings.
3 Why do you think the ridge is forested? Why is the caravan site on the ridge rather than by the sea?
4 Why might you oppose the development of the moraine for new housing estates?

6 COASTLINE FEATURES

The coastal system

Oceans and seas cover 362 million km^2 or 71% of the total surface of the Earth and they contain 97% of the world's water. Figure 6.1 shows the different oceans in the world. Oceans have a major impact on the Earth's climate as they help moderate world temperatures and they supply the world's water cycle. Ocean currents also transfer heat from the tropical areas towards the poles.

The oceans remain at a fairly constant temperature, with an average annual variation of 10°C. The Persian Gulf has the highest summer temperatures at 35°C. The steady temperature is vital for sea life because great temperature variations prevent feeding, growth and reproduction. If insects are not counted, then 65% of the animal species in the world have their homes in the sea, and they form complex food chains.

Fig. 6.1 *The world's oceans. Calculate the size of the Indian and Atlantic oceans. What are the inputs and outputs of the system?*

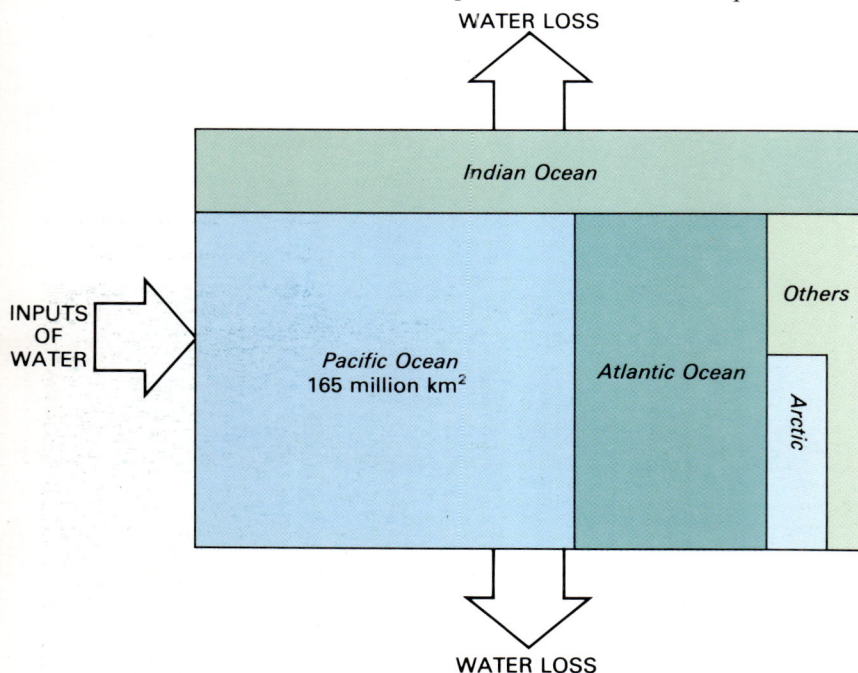

Fig. 6.2 *The ocean food chain*

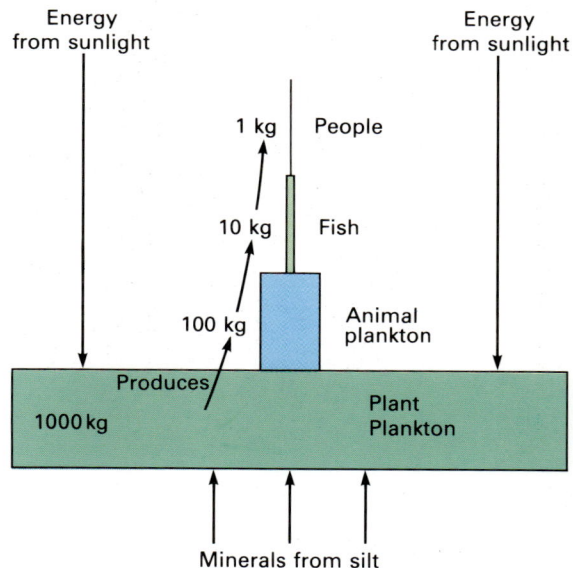

Activities

Figure 6.2 shows a food chain.
1 Why do you think there is a loss in weight between each level in the chain?
2 Why might the dumping of chemical and nuclear waste on the seabed cause serious problems?
3 Imagine you are a campaigner trying to stop the dumping of nuclear waste at sea. Design a poster or leaflet for your campaign. Suggest who might oppose you and for what reasons.

Coastal variations

Coastlines vary in their shape, depth or height, length and appearance, and the appearance of a coastal area is controlled by a number of factors.

Rock type

Soft rocks are more easily worn away and so form lower, gentler areas. Tough, hard rocks resist wave and weather attacks and so form steep headlands and cliffs. Rocks also vary in their structure. If a rock has faults, beds, bands of different hardness or joints, then the sea can attack these areas of weakness and so leave the harder areas standing out, as shown in the photograph (fig. 6.3), taken on Marloes Sands in Dyfed.

Fig. 6.3 *Three chimneys, Marloes Sands, Dyfed*

Activities

Look at figs 6.5 and 6.6.
1 List four differences shown between the two coastlines.
2 Imagine that you are planning a holiday along one of these coastal areas. Which area would you choose and why?
3 Which coastal area do you think would produce the greatest problems for the people living there?

Fig. 6.4 *Energy inputs*

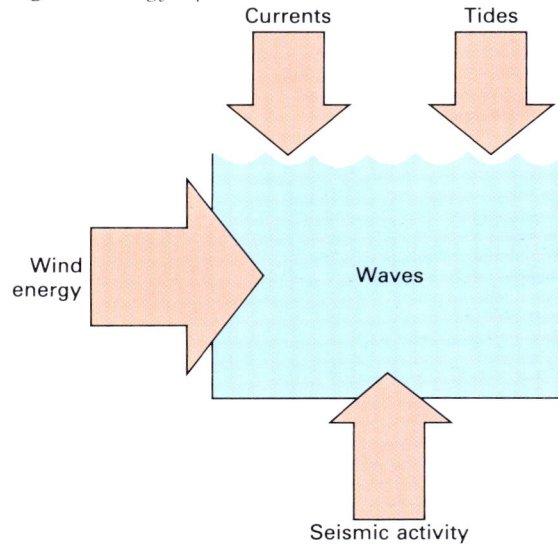

Fig. 6.5 *South Devon*

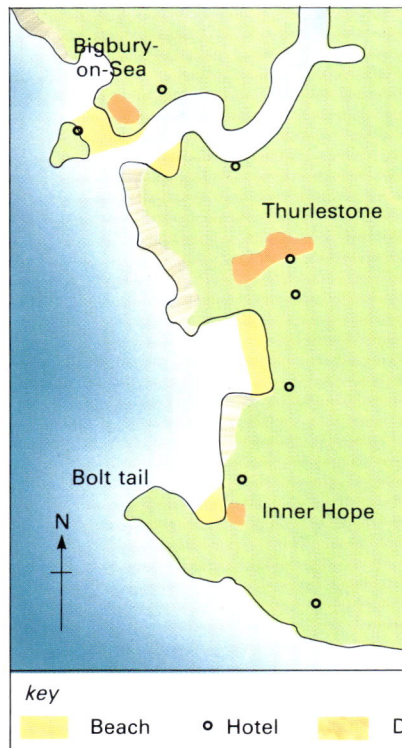

Fig. 6.6 *North-east Norfolk*

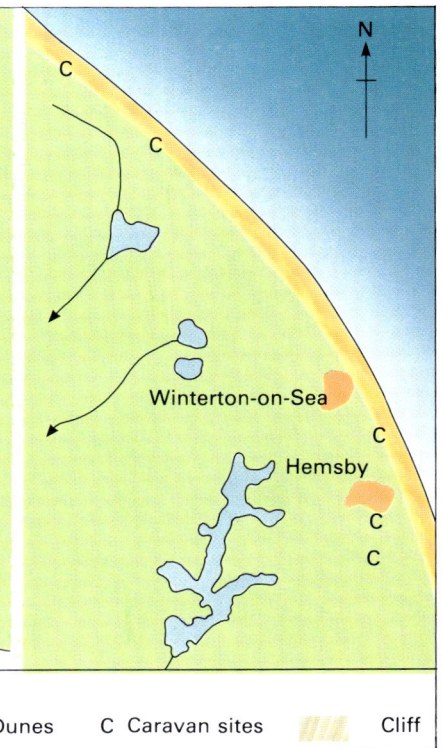

key

Beach   ○ Hotel   Dunes   C Caravan sites   Cliff

The type and size of waves

Oceans receive energy from a number of sources, as shown in fig. 6.4. Over 80% of the energy comes from the drag of the wind on the surface of the water, thus the strength of the wave depends partly on the strength of the wind. Waves rarely exceed 10 m in height but in hurricanes they have been over 21 m. The length of ocean over which the wind can drag the water, called the fetch, is also important. Figure 6.7 shows that the waves hitting the west coast of Britain have a longer distance in which to pick up energy than those reaching the east coast.

The waves in the Atlantic are rarely over 12 m in height but in the larger Pacific they can reach 15 m. The table (fig. 6.8) shows the result of fieldwork in north Norfolk and Pembrokeshire. The difference between the two sets of results is explained partly by the prevailing wind direction, which in the case of the British Isles is from the south-west, which is also the longest fetch.

Fig. 6.7 *The fetch of the British Isles*

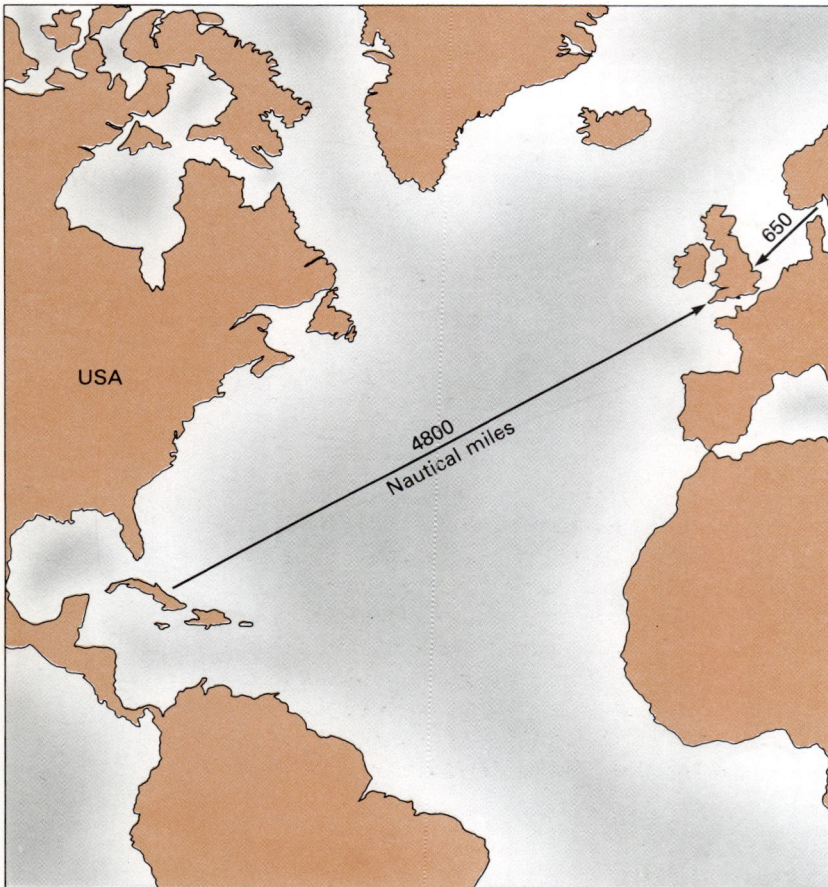

Fig. 6.8 *Wave heights*

Wind direction	Cromer, Norfolk	St David's Head, Dyfed
N	1.5 m	1 m
NE	2.0 m	1 m
SW	0.5 m	3 m
S	0.5 m	1 m

The shape of the wave is also important. Look at fig. 6.9. When a wave enters shallow water it becomes unstable and breaks. Water rushes up the beach (swash) and then returns down the beach (backwash). The shape of the breaking wave is vital. A plunging breaker comes down on the coastline from some height and so energy is fed into backwash more than into swash. This leads to the removal of material from the coastline.

Fig. 6.9 *Wave shapes. Why will a spilling breaker add material to the coastline?*

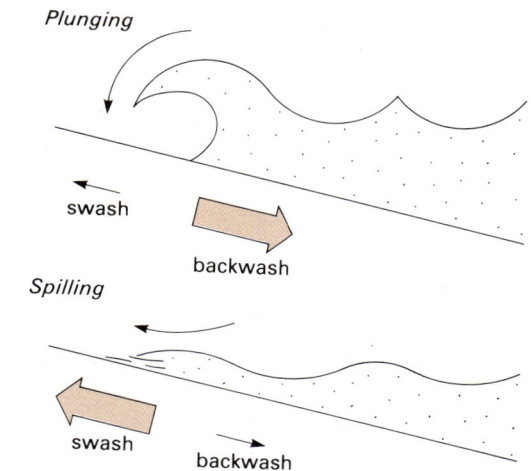

Wave and coastline direction

If a wave hits the coastline directly, then all of its energy can be used directly in the coastline but if it hits at an angle it is less effective. At an angle, more of the wave energy is lost in

Activities

Study fig. 6.10.
1 Suggest why there is no sand at B. Where do you think it has gone?
2 Why do you think such a movement of sand is a major problem for human activity?
3 How would you measure the speed and direction of the sand movement?
4 How do you think features A and C have been formed?

Fig. 6.10 *Hengistbury Head, Dorset*

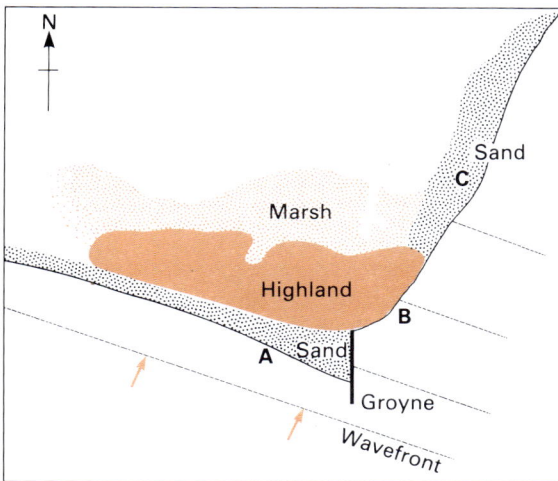

coming on shore. Frequently the wavefront
bends in shallow water so losing more energy.
The direction of the wave may be altered as it
comes onshore. It is slowed down by shallow
water and so a wave may be bent, as shown in
fig. 6.11. This is called wave refraction.

Fig. 6.11 *Wave refraction. What effect will this have on
the headland?*

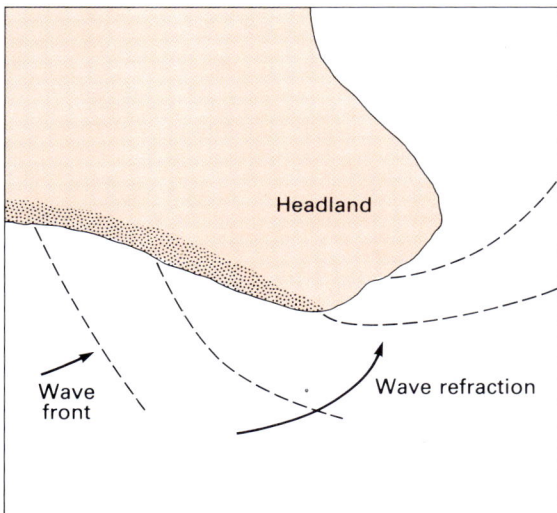

Tidal range and depth of water

Shallow water causes waves to break and so
lose their energy. Deep water allows waves to
bring all their energy directly onto the
coastline. Figure 6.12 shows two different tidal
ranges. The sea-level is rising around the
world as the ice caps melt. This may well
increase the rate of coastal erosion. Large tidal
ranges, such as the 1.5 km horizontal range at
Weston-super-Mare, cause major problems for
shipping and tourism.

Fig. 6.12 *Tidal range. Measure the difference in the area
attacked by the sea. Which coastline would be eroded more
by the sea? Explain your answer*

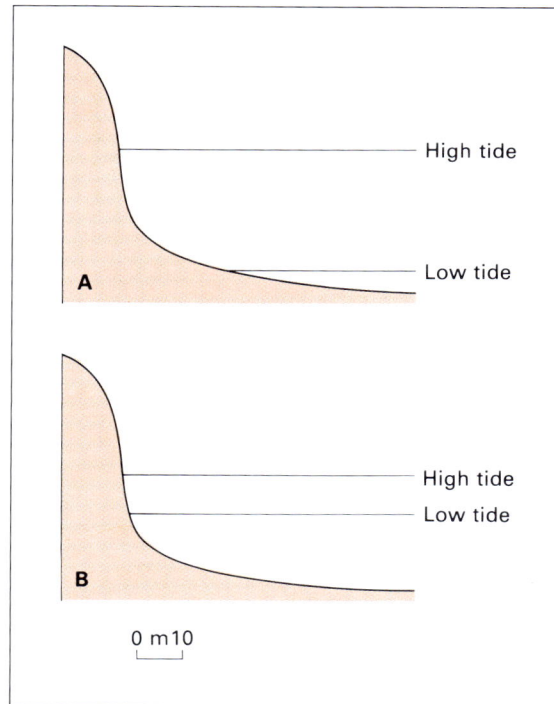

Other processes

Coastlines are also influenced by processes
other than wave action. Weathering, the work
of rivers, wind, landslides and the work of ice
all influence the appearance of the coastline.
Even animal life can have an impact on
coastlines. The Great Barrier Reef in Australia
is the largest coral reef in the world. It forms a
2012 km breakwater down the east coast of
Australia and reaches 500 m in thickness. This
acts to protect the coast behind from storm
waves.

Human activity

This can remove parts of the coast, add to it or
exploit the advantages offered by coastal
locations.

Time

Why do you think this factor is such an
important influence? With time, the sea has
longer to wear down rocks and widen any
weakness. Coasts exposed to the sea for a long
time are worn down with many islands and
beaches.

Sea erosion

Fig. 6.13 *A natural arch – Newgale Sands, Dyfed. Draw a sketch of it and label the various areas that you think are influenced by the different processes of marine erosion*

The processes

The sea uses its energy to wear away the coastline. Stones are picked up by the waves and hurled at the coastline. This is called coastal abrasion. These stones stay low in the water and so tend to undercut features. The broken-off fragments of rock collide and are broken down still further into fine sand. This process is called attrition. The sheer weight of falling water can break rocks. In storms the pressure of the falling water may exceed 8000 kg/m^2. Air may be compressed in cracks in the rock and force them apart. Also some rocks dissolve in sea water. This is called solution and is common in lime-rich rocks. The photograph (fig. 6.13) shows a natural arch and much evidence of the different erosion processes. The sea erodes any weakness in the rocks to form caves, arches, bays and cliffs.

Caves

The shape, size and appearance of a cave will partly depend on the type and direction of the weakness in the rock. If the weakness is vertical then a tall, often thin cave is produced, as in fig. 6.14, along a fault. If the weakness is horizontal then a slit cave is produced, which is low but wide, as in the cave in fig. 6.15 which is eroded along a weak bed of rock. Most erosion of caves occurs during storms when waves have a great deal of energy.

Fig. 6.14 *Fault cave*

Fig. 6.15 *Bed cave, Durdle Door, Dorset*

Arches

Sometimes the weakness goes through a headland and so caves form at both ends and get bigger until they meet. This produces a natural arch. Look at the photograph (fig. 6.16) of Durdle Door in Dorset. As the arch is gradually widened its top can no longer be supported and so it falls. This leaves the far side of the arch as an isolated pillar of rock called a stack.

Bays

If a weak area of rock exists the sea may erode further inland to form an inlet in the coast. If this process works on a large scale a bay is formed.

Fig. 6.16 *Durdle Door, Dorset. What do you think the weakness was in this case?*

Activities

Look at fig. 6.17 which shows Swanage Bay in Dorset.
1 Measure how far each bay has been eroded compared to the headland A. Why is there a difference between the bays?
2 What evidence would you look for to prove that headland A is being eroded more than the bays?
3 Imagine you are a land developer. Design a poster advertising your new properties for sale at location B on the map stressing the physical attraction of the site.

The type of coast shown in fig. 6.17, with the bands of rock at 90° to the coast, is called an atlantic coastline.

Smaller versions of bays are coves and sometimes the inlet is so narrow that it forms a slit in the coastline called a geo. In the case of Lulworth Cove in Dorset, (fig. 6.18), the coastline is called Pacific as the bands of rock lie parallel to the coastline (similar to the west coast of America). In this case, weaker areas in the outer band of limestone were cut through so the sea could wear away the softer clay behind.

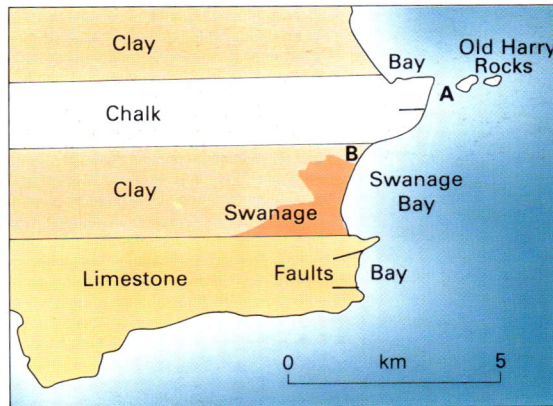

Fig. 6.17 *Swanage Bay, Dorset*

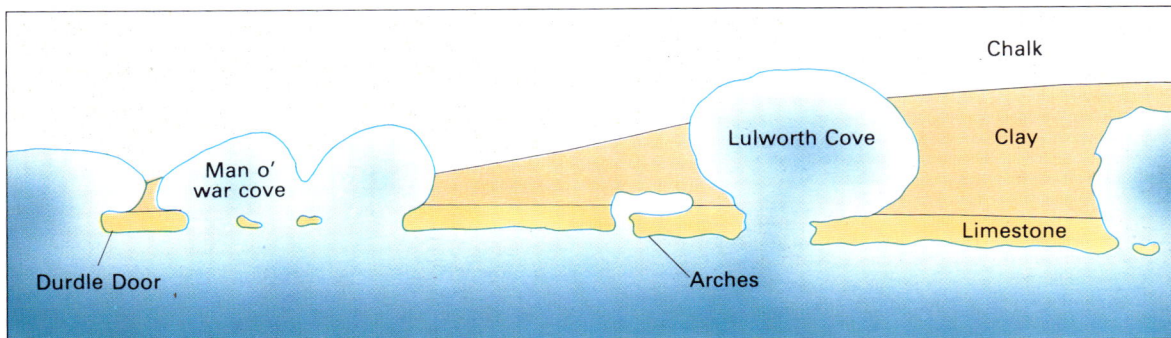

Fig. 6.18 *Lulworth Cove area of Dorset. What will eventually happen to the coastline as the clay is eroded?*

Fig. 6.19 *Limestone cliffs*

Fig. 6.20 *Wave-cut platform*

Fig. 6.21 *Southern part of the Isle of Wight. What effects do you think the 1928 landslide at Niton had on human activity?*

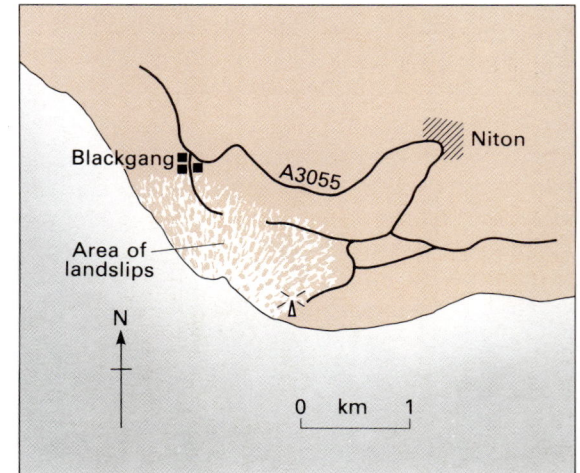

Cliffs

These are steep slopes which sometimes have distinct ledges because the sea has eroded softer beds or weaknesses. Different rock types will often produce different slope angles. Jointed and bedded rocks produce stepped or angular cliffs, as shown in fig. 6.19. The slopes are kept steep by the sea undercutting at the foot. As it undercuts, so an area of uneroded rock remains at the base of the cliff, which is exposed at low tide as a wave-cut platform, like the one in fig. 6.20.

Weathering is concentrated on the cliff top and works towards reducing the angle of the cliff. If the effect of the sea at the foot of the cliff is reduced, a gentle cliff will form.

If the rock is soft and is easily wetted, then it will tend to slip and slide and may even contain so much water that it flows like a muddy river. This mass movement produces a gentler cliff angle, or one with distinct ledges along the line of the slip. These landslides and slips can have a major impact on human activity. Figure 6.21 shows part of the southern area of the Isle of Wight. In 1928 a vast landslide over 150 m wide occurred west of Niton. The whole of the southern coastline of the Isle of Wight is subject to landslips because the underlying rock is clay.

Effects of coastal erosion

Ports and resorts

Erosion creates headlands and bays. The headlands provide shelter for ports and seaside resorts. The map (fig. 6.22) shows part of east Kent. Margate and Broadstairs became holiday resorts with their sandy sheltered beaches. Their growth was made possible by the building of a rail link to London in the mid-nineteenth century. Before that, they were reached by coastal steamers and so Margate, with a nearer location to London, had an advantage over Broadstairs. Broadstairs and Ramsgate are both small fishing ports and Ramsgate's sheltered harbour is a ferry terminal for crossings to Calais in France. More recently the need for sheltered harbours has been less vital and so new ferry ports have developed on flat coastlines such as the hoverport at Pegwell Bay.

Fig. 6.22 *East Kent*

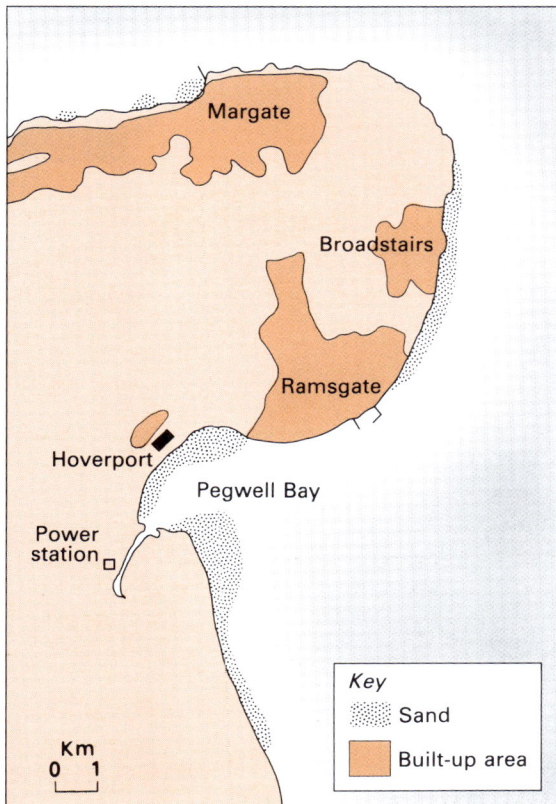

Key

Sand

Built-up area

Fishing

Many sheltered bays are ideal for fishing, especially for shallow-water types such as plaice and sole. Often these areas are sources of valuable crabs and lobsters.

Defence

Headlands caused by coastal erosion have also been used for defence, for example at Scarborough. The castle was built on the headland as the steep cliffs gave protection on three sides from attack.

Mining

Marine erosion may expose mineral seams in cliff faces. In Dyfed the cliffs are full of tunnels and shafts used for mining coal. The coal was loaded directly into ships to be transported to other areas. Today these shafts can cause accidents to careless holidaymakers. In other areas such as Portland in Dorset, marine erosion has exposed quarry stone of high quality. This could be loaded directly into boats, as shown by the crane in the photograph (fig. 6.23). Marine erosion helped by creating deep water close to the shore but it was still a dangerous activity.

Fig. 6.23 *Portland Bill, Dorset*

Human influence on erosion

Coastlines

Careless human activity can accelerate the rate of erosion by changing the depth of water and increasing the supply of material used for erosion.

Look at fig. 6.24, the headland was quarried for iron stone in the 1850s, and offshore dredging for iron ore was carried out. The effect was massive erosion of the now weakened headland by powerful waves. In 1938 a breakwater was built to reduce the loss of sand from Bournemouth. This prevented sand from protecting the foot of the cliff.

It is more usual for human activity to protect coastlines from erosion at the cliff foot, on the cliff face or over the whole stretch of coastline.

Fig. 6.24 *Hengistbury Head, Dorset. What effect has the breakwater had on nearby Christchurch harbour?*

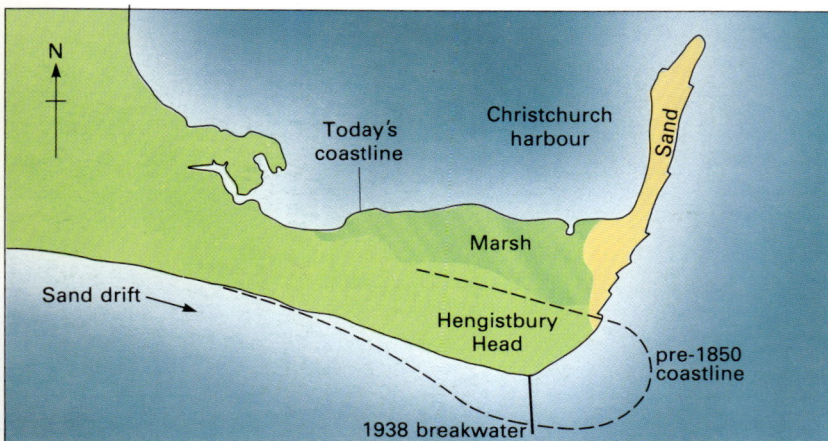

Barton-on-Sea, Hampshire

The problem here is that:
1 the rock is soft and easily eroded;
2 water soaks through the gravel and builds up in the silt zone forming springs which cut valleys and cause landslides;
3 weathering wears down the cliff top; and
4 Barton-on-Sea is in the centre of a wide bay and is open to wave attack.

Fig. 6.25 *The problem at Barton*

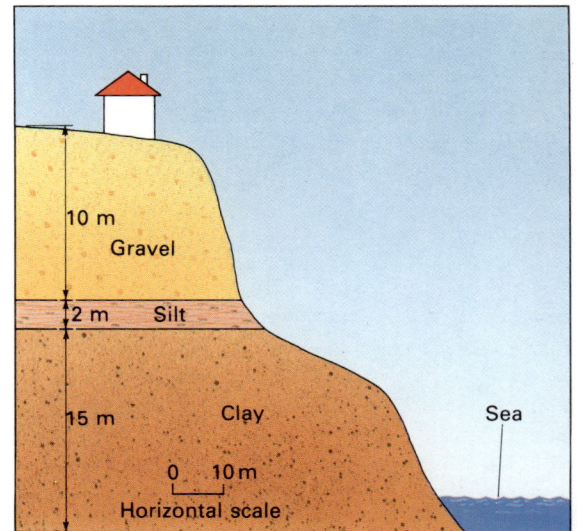

Fig. 6.26 *The solutions at Barton*

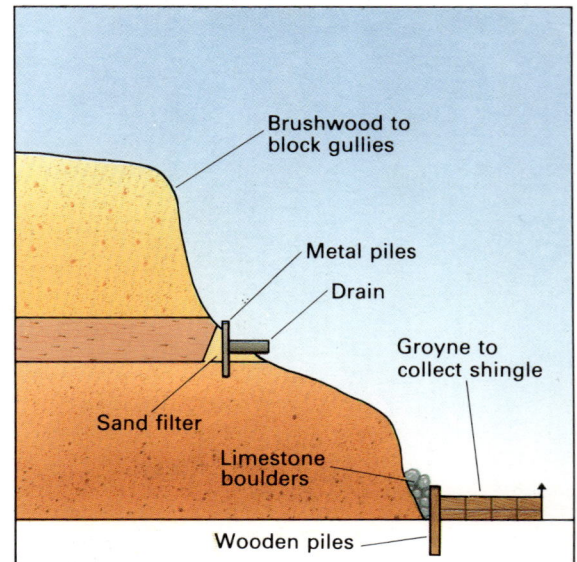

Activities

Study fig. 6.25.
1 How high is the cliff? How far is the edge from the building shown? If the cliff slips 1 m each year, how long before the building has vanished down the cliff?
2 Barton-on-Sea is a holiday resort. In what way do you think visitors may speed up cliff erosion?

Study fig. 6.26.
3 How was the cliff foot protected from erosion?
4 Sheet piles were driven into the cliff face and a drain built. Explain what this was designed to control.
5 Look at the photograph (fig. 6.27). List the evidence that shows that the scheme has had mixed results.

Fig. **6.27** *Barton beach 1986*

A failure to look at both cliff and cliff-foot processes can produce poor defences. Sheringham in Norfolk has a sea defence of a stout wooden barrier designed to absorb the energy of the waves and groynes to collect drifting shingle. But the cliff still retreats, as shown in fig. 6.28. Look at fig. 6.29 which is a map of the coast in the area.

Estuaries

Sometimes estuaries need to be protected. Much of the Thames estuary has had sea defences built to reduce the risk of erosion and flooding. The defences consist of a series of sea walls and flood barriers, as shown in fig. 6.30. These were built to prevent another disaster like the one in 1953, when a North Sea surge came over the existing defences and flooded a large area of eastern England. On Canvey Island fifty-eight people were drowned as the whole island was covered in water. Many of the estuaries along the east coast of Britain are under threat from flooding by especially high tides, because the area is slowly sinking and the melting ice caps are causing a steady rise in the sea-level of 10 mm every ten years.

Fig. **6.28** *Coastal defences Norfolk*

Fig. **6.29** *Field plan, West Runton, Norfolk. Why do you think the sea defences vary along the stretch of coastline?*

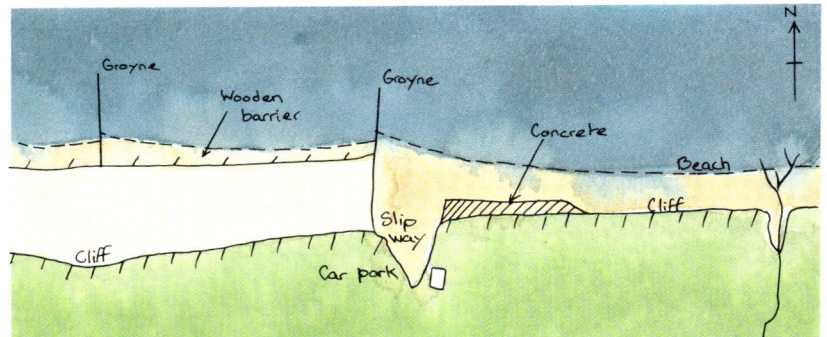

Fig. **6.30** *Thames flood defences. Why did the building of the Thames flood barrier at Woolwich force the raising of the sea walls along the Essex and Kent coasts? Why do you think the building of such defences might increase the rate of estuary erosion.*

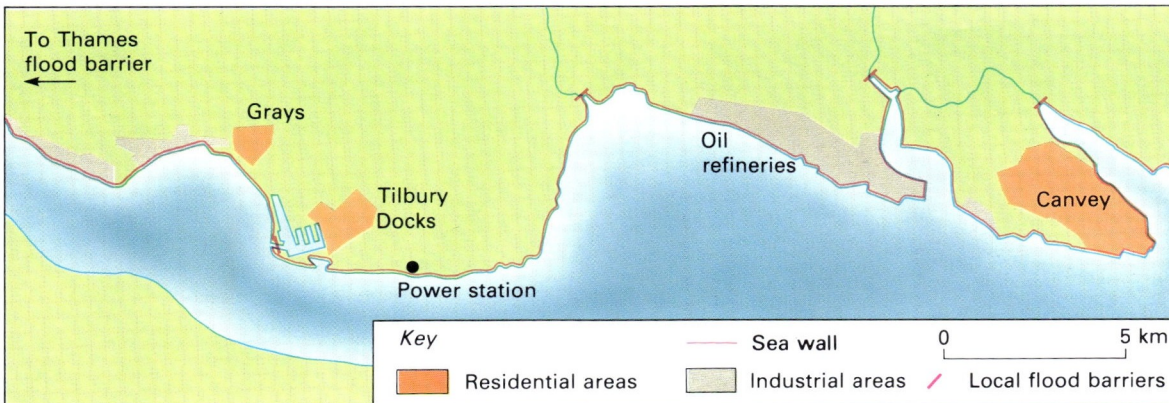

The supervision of coastlines

Coastlines have to be carefully managed as the pressure on their use is increasing. Many of the activities in the Pembrokeshire coast National Park area are in conflict. Look at fig. 6.31 which shows many of these activities and conflicts.

In 1952, 270 km of the Pembrokeshire coast was designated a national park, including the Pembrokeshire Coastal footpath. The main objectives of the Park Authority was to balance the various demands upon the area. Figure 6.32 shows the rugged scenery that attracts about 130 000 staying visitors on a peak-season day, yet 2700 ha are also used for firing ranges by the Ministry of Defence, and Milford Haven is one of the biggest oil ports in Britain!

Fig. 6.31 *Coastal pressures and conflicts. Suggest why swimming and fishing might conflict. Why do you think industry and wildlife preservation are in conflict?*

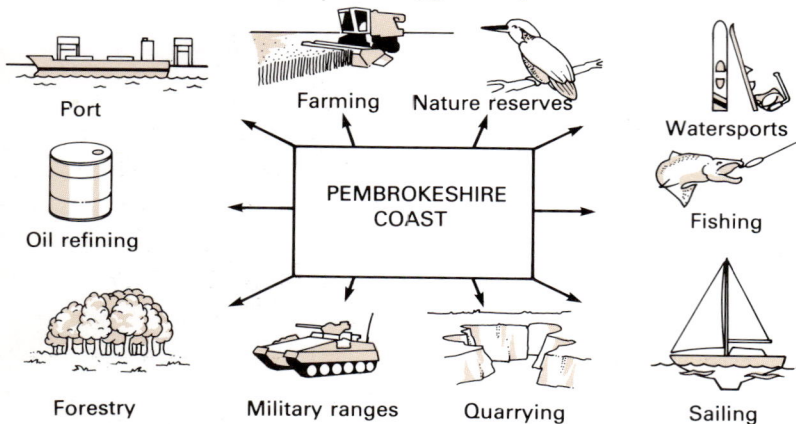

Port
Oil refining
Forestry
Farming
Nature reserves
Military ranges
Quarrying
Watersports
Fishing
Sailing

PEMBROKESHIRE COAST

Fig. 6.32 *Pembrokeshire Coast National Park*

The Authority's policy

1 *Preserve and enhance natural beauty*
Why do you think that this is so difficult to carry out?
2 *Provide recreation opportunities*
In 1984 over 1.3 million people visited the park and spent over £150 million in the area. Considering that 93% of these visitors arrive by car many of the provisions have to be to help parking and traffic flow. This objective may clash with the first objective.
3 *Conservation of wildlife*
This area has a number of important bird reserves including Skomer Island. Many of the beaches are visited by grey seals.
4 *Provide facilities for the local population*
This can produce conflicts. Much of the area is farmland and modern farming techniques of mechanisation, use of chemicals and removal of hedges threaten both wildlife and the beauty of the landscape. But farming does offer local employment and is vital to produce food. The table (6.33) shows many of the activities that, in turn, are problems for farmers. Similarly road building and industry are needed to help the local population.

Fig. 6.33 *Effects of the coastal foot-path on agriculture. Source: Pembrokeshire National Parks Authority*

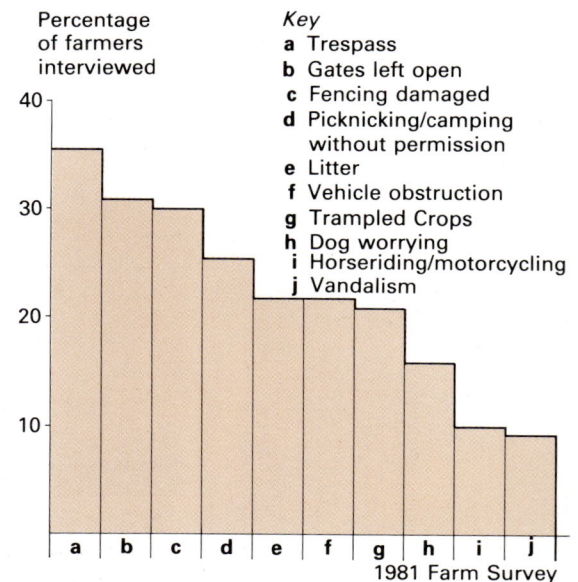

Percentage of farmers interviewed

Key
a Trespass
b Gates left open
c Fencing damaged
d Picknicking/camping without permission
e Litter
f Vehicle obstruction
g Trampled Crops
h Dog worrying
i Horseriding/motorcycling
j Vandalism

1981 Farm Survey

The Authority's solution

Part of the problem is the very varied nature of coastal activities, as shown in fig. 6.34. The Authority has decided to develop 'honey-pot' sites. These are sites chosen for development and exploitation in an attempt to concentrate the visitors in a few areas and so save the other unspoiled areas. These sites are shown in figure 6.35.

Fig. 6.34 *Activities of the coastal foot-path users. Source: Pembrokeshire Coast Path Authority report*

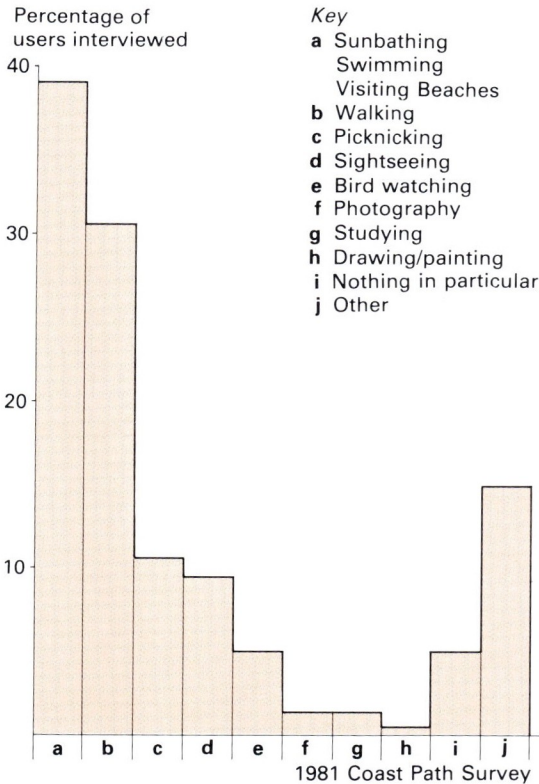

Percentage of users interviewed

Key
a Sunbathing
  Swimming
  Visiting Beaches
b Walking
c Picnicking
d Sightseeing
e Bird watching
f Photography
g Studying
h Drawing/painting
i Nothing in particular
j Other

1981 Coast Path Survey

Fig. 6.35 *Pembrokeshire Coast National Park. What facilities would you develop at the centres designated for expansion?*

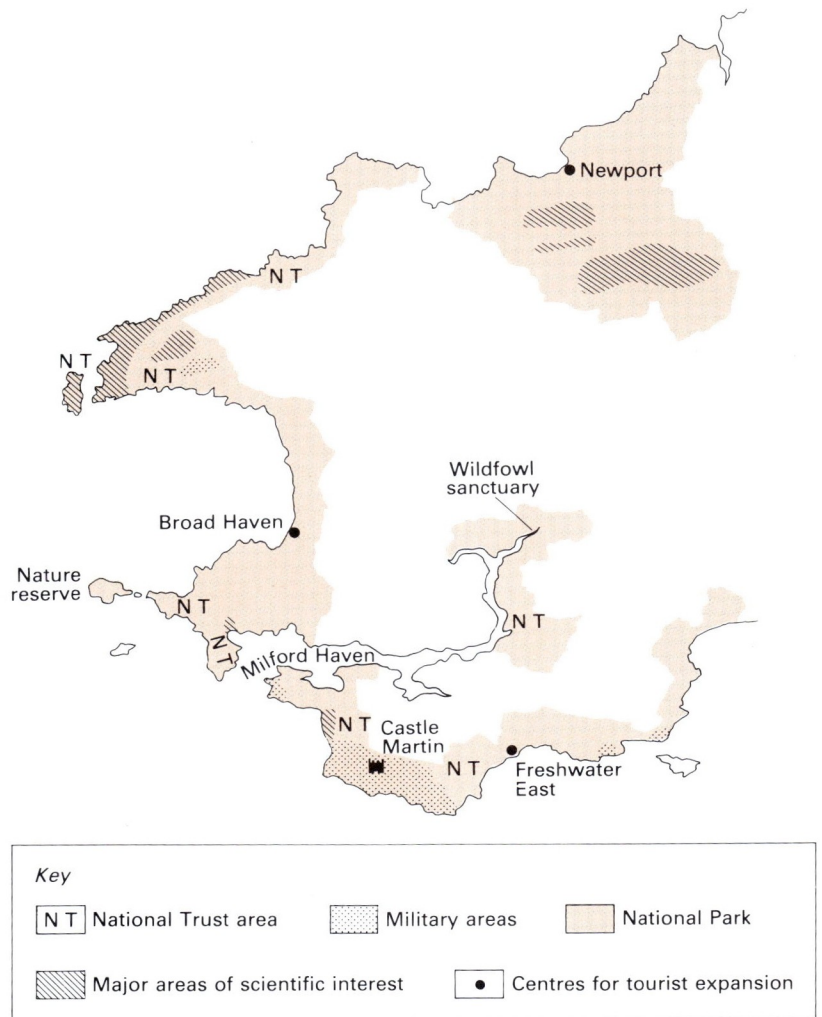

Key

N T National Trust area   Military areas   National Park

Major areas of scientific interest   ● Centres for tourist expansion

Fig. 6.36 *National Park Authority expenditure*

	Net expenditure	1984	1986
A	Conservation	14.1	18.5
B	Town and country planning	10.1	10.1
C	Interpretation and information	19.3	16.9
D	Recreation	22.9	23.0
E	Support to local community	1.4	1.5
F	Management and administration	32.1	30.0
		100.0	100.0

Activities

1 Look at the table (fig. 6.36) which shows the 1986 expenditures by the Park Authority. Draw a diagram of the 1986 figures. Calculate the changes from the 1984 figures. Try to explain the changes in expenditure shown.
2 Imagine that the Ministry of Defence agrees to give up the ranges at Castle Martin (fig. 6.35). This area has to be integrated into the Park. Suggest what ideas and arguments might be put forward by
   a a wildlife conservation officer;
   b the developer of a tourist complex; and
   c a local resident.

Differing marine deposits

Fig. 6.37 *Beach ridges, Blakeney point, Norfolk*

Fig. 6.38 *Dune erosion*

Variations in angle

Beaches vary in their area and angle depending upon the type of material that is deposited. Coarse pebbles produce steep beaches and sand produces gentle beaches.

Beaches tend to have the largest stones at the top because they have been thrown there by storm waves and cannot be removed by weaker normal waves. The smallest stones and sand are usually washed down to the foot of the beach, where attrition in the surf zone makes them smaller.

Most beaches have distinct levels, shown by strand lines of driftwood and seaweed or by ridges of coarser stones. Figure 6.37 shows three such levels. These are formed by different tide levels. The highest is usually a spring high tide in storm conditions and so material at this level is rarely moved.

In some areas, extensive dune belts have formed, as sand exposed at low tide is blown inland by onshore winds. This sand collects around obstacles and may build up to form dunes that eventually merge into large ridges.

Fig. 6.39 *Beach transect, Holkham, Norfolk*

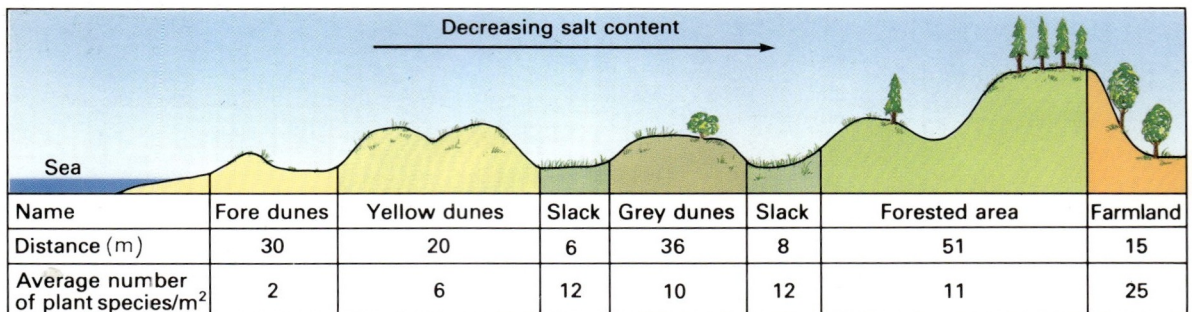

Name	Fore dunes	Yellow dunes	Slack	Grey dunes	Slack	Forested area	Farmland
Distance (m)	30	20	6	36	8	51	15
Average number of plant species/m²	2	6	12	10	12	11	25

Activities

Look at the transect (fig. 6.39) of Holkham Beach, Norfolk.
1 Draw a bar or line graph to show the changing number of plant species up the beach. Explain why this pattern occurs and why the plant types are different in the slacks.
2 What differences would you expect between the plants at the start and at the end of the transect?
3 Look at fig. 6.38 which shows the impact of human activity on a dune area. What is the value of protecting such areas? Design a dune protection plan for Holkham Beach.

Fig. 6.40 *Part of the north Norfolk coast. Why do you think gaps have appeared in the bar?*

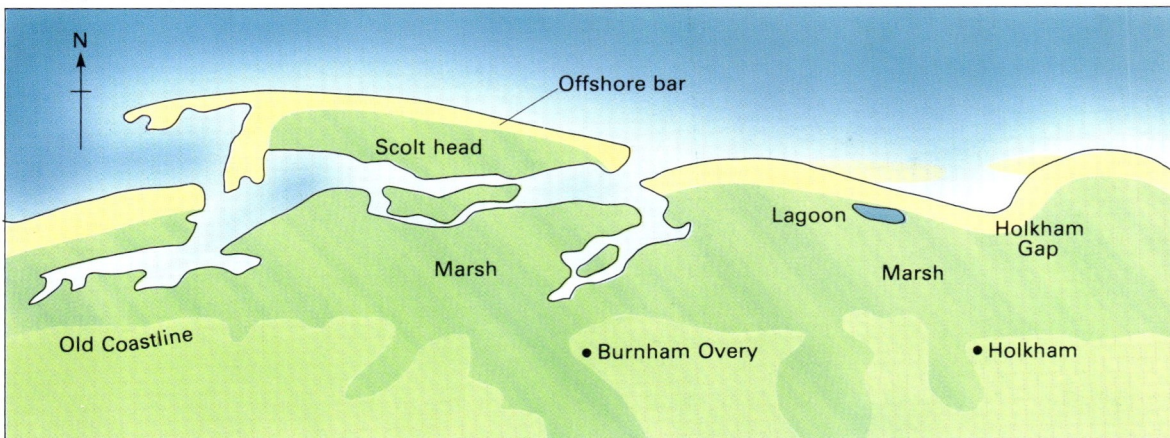

Variations in plan

At the end of the last ice age the sea-level began to rise and so pushed eroded material onshore. This created a series of vast offshore bars. In some cases, as shown in fig. 6.40, they remain as islands but in others they have been pushed right onshore and can trap weak rivers to form lagoons. Figure 6.41, the lagoon trapped behind the bar has become overgrown by marsh vegetation and now makes a natural bird reserve.

In other cases movement has occurred along the coast when waves wash on to the beach at an angle. Look at fig. 6.42. Material is pushed up the beach by the force of the wave but then it is pulled back down the beach under the influence of gravity. Thus there is a difference between the angle of upwash and of backwash and so material moves along the beach. Figure 6.43 shows a groyne on a beach. Coastal

Fig. 6.42 *Longshore drift*

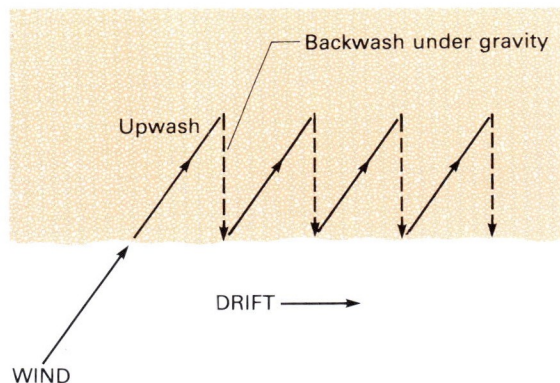

Fig. 6.41 *Bay bar, Weybourne, Norfolk*

authorities build these to slow the drift and keep beach material from drifting away.

Fig. 6.43 *Beach groyne, showing the effect of longshore drift.*

Fig. 6.44 *Mid-Wales Coast. In what direction do you think drift is moving? What effect has it had on the river*

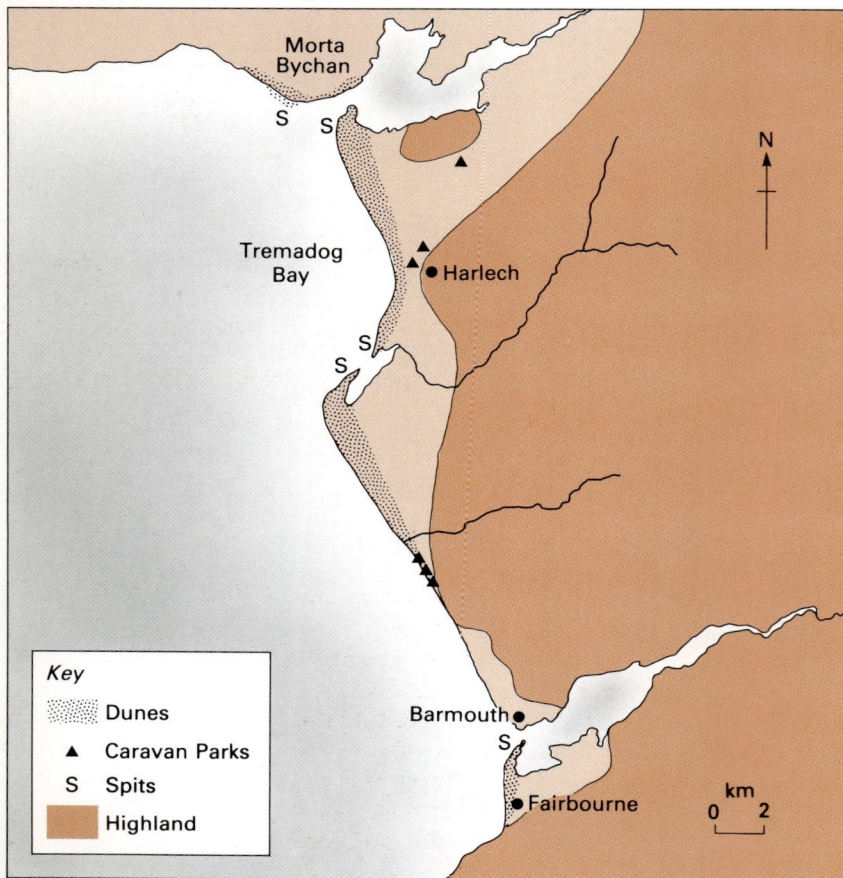

Key
: Dunes
▲ Caravan Parks
S Spits
▨ Highland

Fig. 6.45 *Hurst Castle spit. What is the evidence that this has been turned several times in the past?*

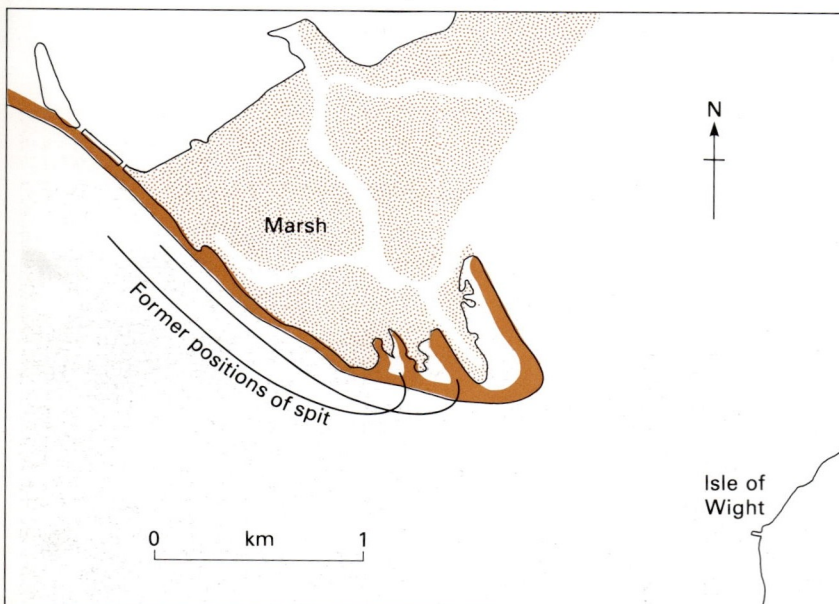

The movement of material along the coast causes the formation of spits. These projecting areas of sand and gravel are formed when the direction of the coastline suddenly changes, as long as the water is shallow and there is a supply of material. Figure 6.44 shows a line of spits along the Welsh coast. These coastal deposits have created many opportunities for the development of holiday resorts like Barmouth. Changing wind direction or the bending effect of waves as they swing round the end of the spit may cause this end to turn or hook. Figure 6.45 shows Hurst Castle spit in Hampshire.

Sometimes drift may push a spit out to join an island to the mainland. This is called a tombolo. The photograph (fig. 6.46) shows Chesil Bank which joins the mainland of Dorset to the Isle of Portland. Suggest an alternative method for the formation of tombolos such as Chesil Beach.

Fig. 6.46 *Chesil Bank, Dorset*

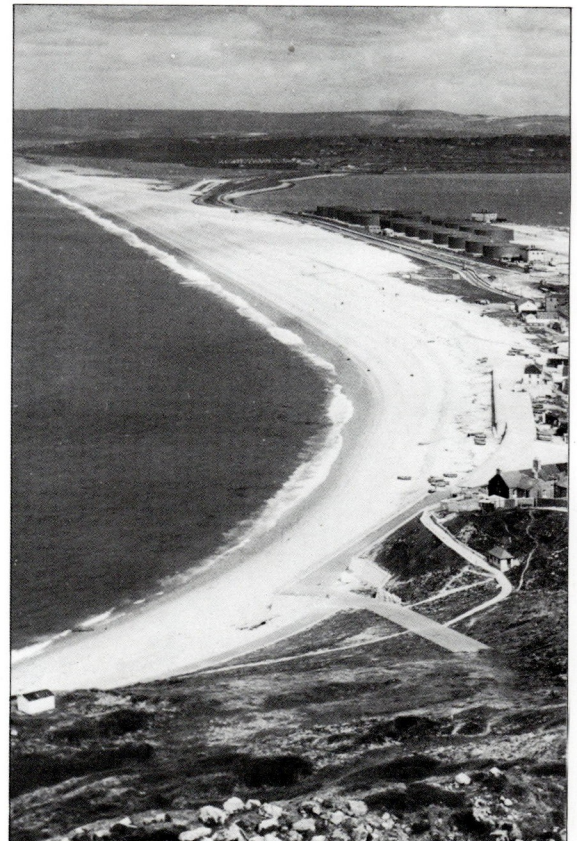

Marine deposits and economic activity

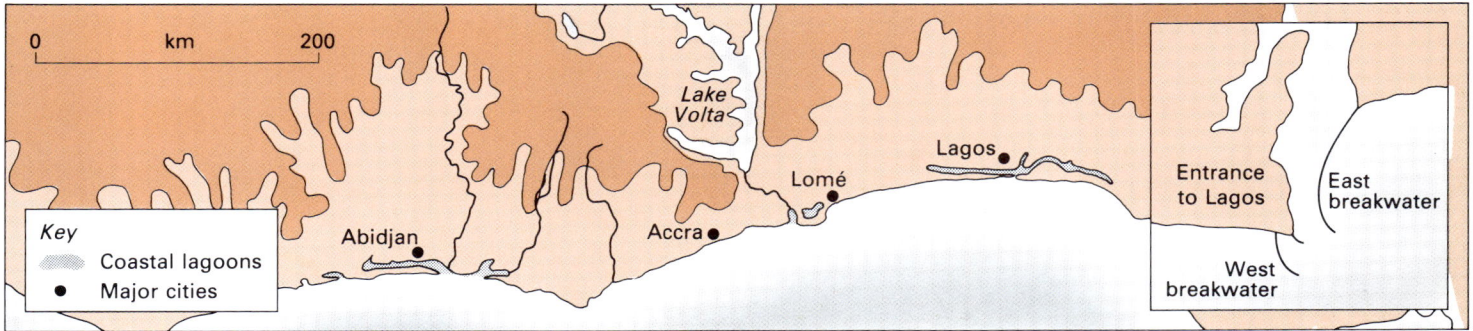

Fig. 6.47 *Coastline of West Africa*

Ports

Some areas have been affected by marine deposition. Coastal sand bars and coral reefs have prevented the development of large ports along the west coast of Africa, (fig. 6.47). Lagos grew up because it was in one of the few gaps through the coastal barrier, but extensive breakwaters have had to be built and constantly extended to prevent the gap becoming blocked. What effect do you think this has had on the economic development of the area?

Sometimes existing ports may become blocked by deposition. The map (fig. 6.48) shows part of the north Norfolk coast. In medieval times these ports were very prosperous but then a shingle bar caused silting and so today none of these are active ports. There was little effort made to prevent this silting, as there was at Lagos, because there were rival ports to the west. Large parts of these areas of salt marsh are now used for

cattle grazing.

Reclamation

In some areas the natural process of salt-marsh formation has been increased by people reclaiming the land directly from the sea. In the northern Netherlands the Zuider Zee project which started in 1920 added 10% to the land area of the country. Figure 6.49 shows a typical reclaimed polder. Sea walls are built and then the area within is pumped dry. Once the salt is washed out by the rain, the land can be farmed intensively.

Coastal lagoons, mud and sand flats can also be reclaimed for industry and port development.

Fig. 6.48 *Part of the Norfolk coast*

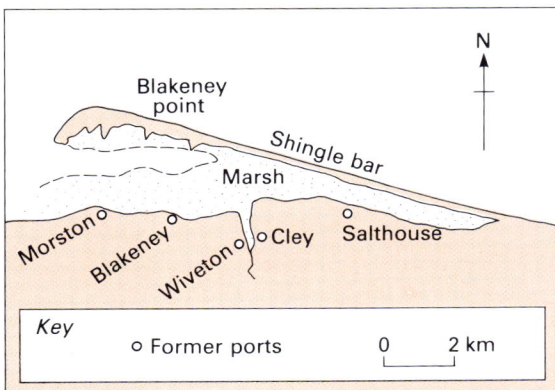

Fig. 6.49 *Polder in Ijsselmeer scheme, Netherlands. In what ways does the polder landscape differ from your landscape?*

Activities

Look at fig. 6.50 which shows the Mediterranean coastline of France.
1 Why do you think the French Government decided to create a string of tourist resorts in 1963? What problems had to be overcome to build this development?
2 In the Marseille area, lagoons have been reclaimed for port and heavy industrial areas. Suggest why these activities might want such reclaimed sites. What groups might oppose these developments and what would be their attitudes?

Fig. 6.50 *Mediterranean coastline of France*

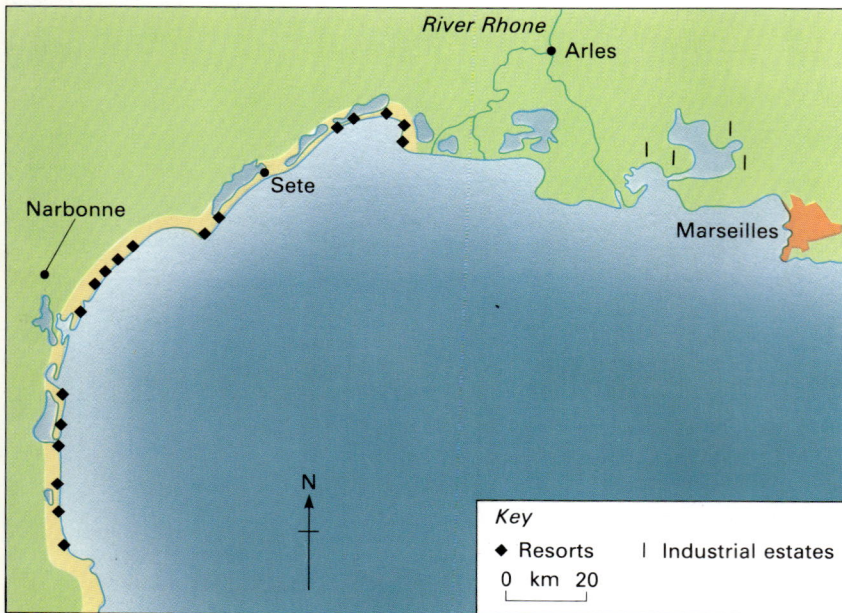

Fig. 6.51 *Cockle dredger, Leigh-on-Sea, Essex*

Fishing

Mudbanks and sandbanks may provide valuable fishing grounds. Many of the North Sea fishing grounds are based on submerged sandbanks. Inshore banks may provide shell-fishing areas like those near Leigh-on-Sea, Essex where cockles and whelks are dredged up, as shown in fig. 6.51. The most prosperous onshore activity was oyster fishing, which reached its greatest production levels in the nineteenth century. Figure 6.52 shows one of the special 'pits'. The oysters were grown on stakes stuck in the mud in the pit.

Fig. 6.52 *Oyster pits. How do you think the 'pit' worked? Why do you think that this industry has almost died out?*

Minerals

In some places large areas of offshore sands and gravels are dredged up for use in the building industry. Sometimes minerals are dredged up from marine deposits, like the tin ore in Malaysia. In the future a whole range of minerals may be obtained from deposits on the continental shelf.

The sea as a resource

The seas and oceans offer a wide range of resources, as shown in fig. 6.53. Countries like Japan and Iceland have limited natural resources and limited farmland and so have had to rely heavily on the sea for resources. Human activity is threatening to damage the delicate balance of the oceans. Some fish have been fished almost to extinction and a ban has had to be put on whale hunting.

Fig. 6.53 *Ocean resources*

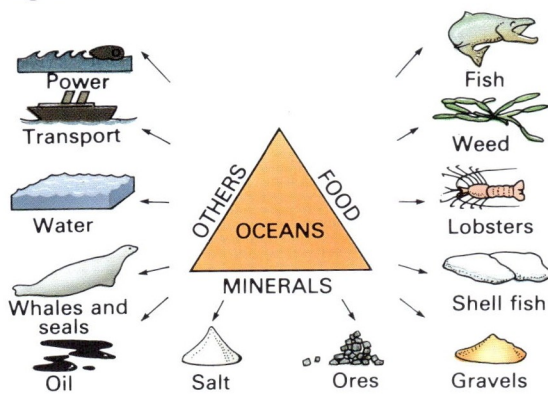

Pollution

There is a vast range of threats from pollution, as shown in fig. 6.54. The map, fig. 6.55, shows part of the Caribbean. This is very vulnerable to environmental damage because it is an area of water which is almost enclosed. Most of the countries that border the sea are developing and so lack the resources to curb

Fig. **6.54** *Threats of pollution. Why is pollution of the sea so difficult to control?*

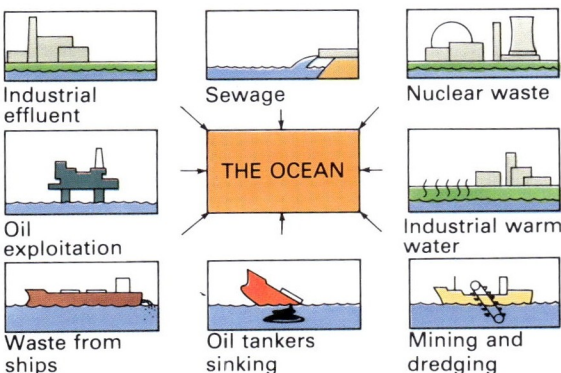

Fig. **6.55** *The Caribbean*

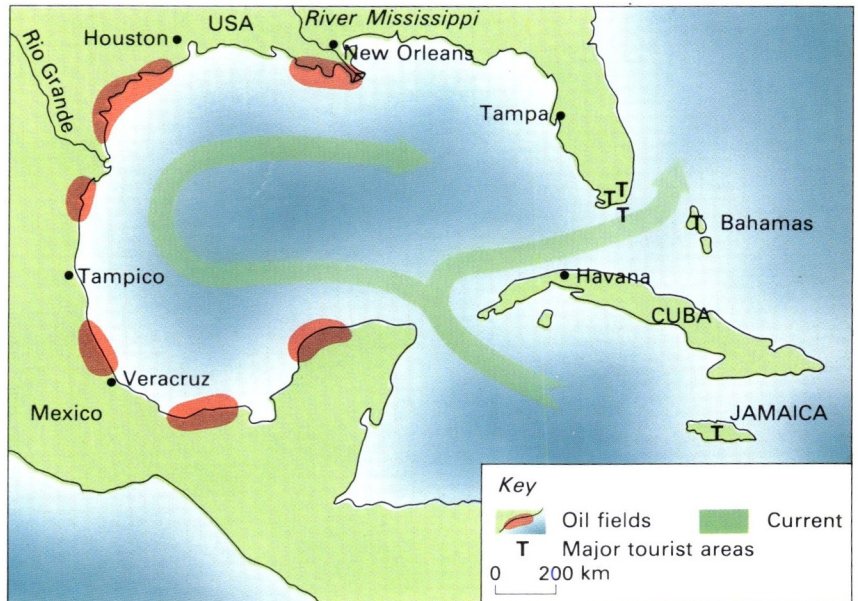

pollution. Much of Mexico's oil extraction is offshore and several major pollution problems have arisen. The political differences in the area further complicate the overall management of the marine resources. The North Sea is another area under threat from pollution.

Political restrictions

Many countries have reacted to threats of overfishing or the need to control and develop offshore minerals by setting up boundaries or limits in the sea. Why has a poor country like Peru declared an exclusive fishing zone extending 900 km out from the coast?

Supervising the sea

Today comprehensive management schemes are being suggested for marine areas such as the North Sea and Mediterranean. Why are these areas well suited to such schemes? Strict controls on sewage and the dumping of industrial waste into the sea have been introduced by the Economic Community. Can you discover why this was particularly necessary in the case of the Mediterranean?

7 THE LANDSCAPE

The landscape system

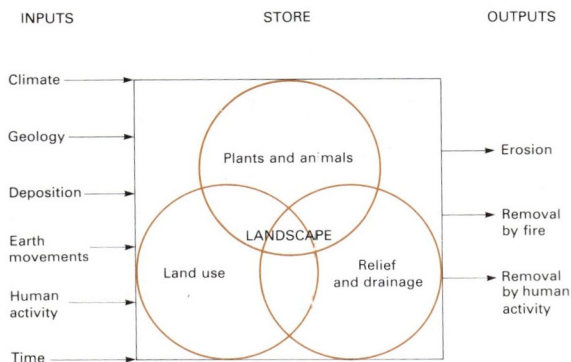

Fig. 7.1 *The landscape system. What do you think would happen to the landscape if there was a great fall in the input of temperature?*

Any landscape is a complex mix of relief, water, plants and animals.

The landscape can be seen as a system of inputs and outputs of energy and material, as shown in fig. 7.1. At any given moment of time the landscape is a store of energy and material in balance. If either the inputs or outputs were to change, then so would the balance and appearance of the landscape. The landscape is constantly changing, but much of this change is now due to the activities of people.

Figure 7.2 shows the changing rate of the impact of human activity. The impact will clearly increase in the future as more of the world's developing countries begin to industrialise. Many of these countries are in the tropics where the complex system of plants and life are even more vulnerable.

Fig. 7.2 *The impact of human activities on the landscape. Why did this increase so greatly after 1800?*

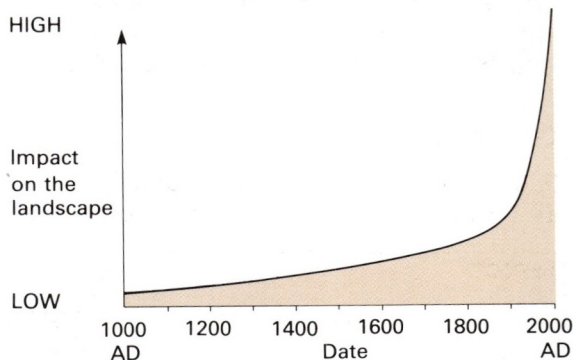

Fig. 7.3 *A landscape in Austria*

Activities

1 Draw a fieldsketch of fig. 7.3 and label the main features of the landscape.
2 Design a way of classifying or grouping the features you have identified. How many features are there in each class or group? Illustrate your answer with a diagram.

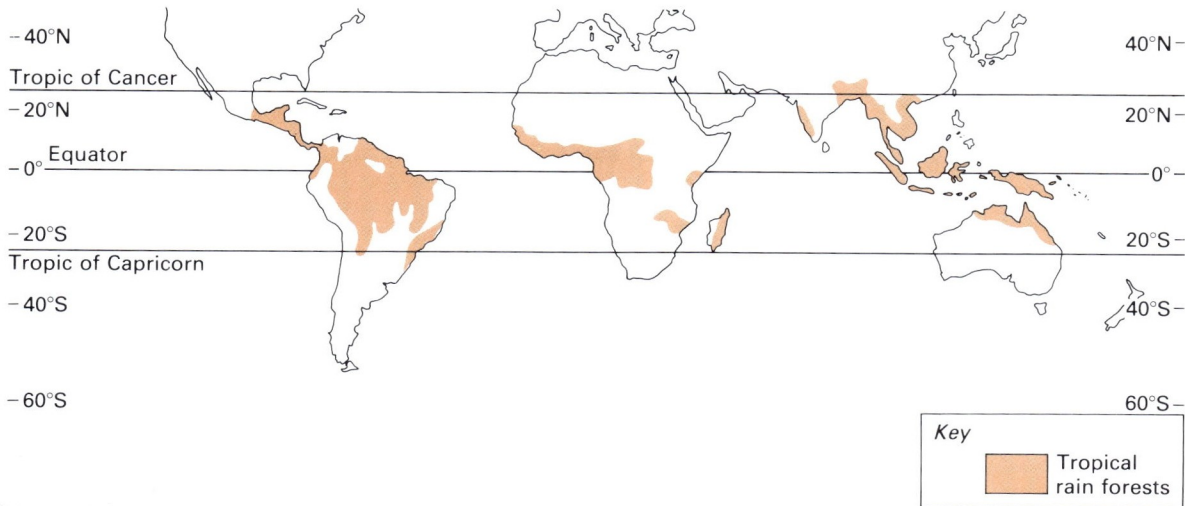

Fig. 7.4 *The World's tropical rainforests*

The world's equatorial rainforests, shown in fig. 7.4, represent the world's richest biological system, but are being cleared at the rate of 40 ha each minute. Human activity is removing the forest to try to gain various resources:

Land for farming

Much is cleared by peasant farmers who cut down the trees and burn them to supply nutrients for subsistence crops. The crop yields soon fall as the soil loses its fertility and so new areas must be cleared to gain food for the growing population. This probably accounts for a loss of 16 million ha each year.

Timber

Tree felling removes 5 million ha each year. The trees are to supply hardwoods which are valuable exports for developing countries.

Grazing land

In parts of Central America and Brazil, forests are burnt and used as pasture for beef cattle to help the protein intake of the population, or to provide valuable exports.

Minerals

Vast areas of forest are cleared to allow opencast iron ore and bauxite mining in the Amazonia area of Brazil. More is cleared to allow roads and railways to be built to transport the ore. These minerals may form the basis of industrial growth in the country.

Reservoirs

The flooding of valleys to provide lakes for irrigation and supply power damage the forest by drowning the trees.

The effect of this clearance is disastrous, as shown in fig. 7.5. In the past it was easier to adjust human activity to fit in with the limits imposed by the landscape. As the use of technology increases, it becomes possible to overcome these limits. Is this a good thing for both the welfare of the landscape and human welfare?

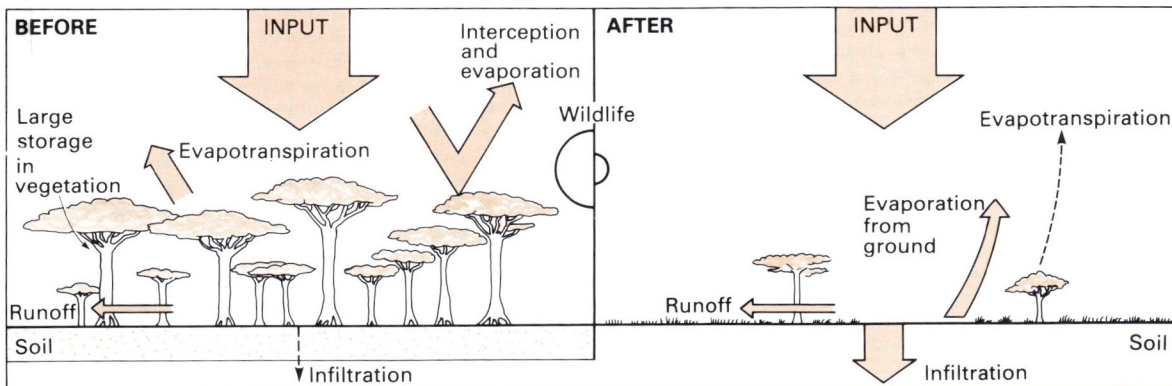

Fig. 7.5 *The impact of forest clearance. What changes have occurred? Why do so many governments still allow forest clearance? How could it affect the world environmental system?*

INDEX

ISBN 0 340 413026

First published 1989

Copyright © 1989 Chris Martin

Photoset by Rowland Phototypesetting Ltd, Bury St Edmunds, Suffolk.
Printed in Hong Kong
for Hodder and Stoughton Educational
a division of Hodder and Stoughton Ltd, Mill Road Dunton Green, Sevenoaks, Kent by Colorcraft Ltd.

ACKNOWLEDGEMENTS

The author and publisher wish to thank the following for permission to reproduce material in this book:

J. Alves, Anglian Water Authority, J. Bedford, M. Dru & R. Thomas, Cleveland County Council, B. E. Vyner (cover photograph), R. Fairhurst, Sally and Richard Greenhill, Icelandic Tourist Board, Lee Valley Park Authority, A. Lintern, D. Melling, Mineral Planning, C. Neilson, J. Owen, Pembrokeshire National Park Authority, B. Silk, L. Tempest, M. Tyler, US Department of the Interior Geological Survey.

933720